The

Daodejing

道德經

of

Laozi

老子

The
Daodejing
道德經
of
Laozi
老子

Translation and Commentary by

Philip J. Ivanhoe

City University of Hong Kong

Hackett Publishing Company, Inc.

Indianapolis/Cambridge

For further information, please address:

> Hackett Publishing Company, Inc.
> P.O. Box 44937
> Indianapolis, IN 46244-0937

> www.hackettpublishing.com

Composition by T. C. Kline III
Cover design by Robyn Sahleen
Seal design by Ho Yen-ch'uan 何炎泉
Printed at Malloy, Inc.

Cover art: Ma Lin, *Scholar Reclining and Watching Rising Clouds,*
detail. © The Cleveland Museum of Art, 2001.

Library of Congress Cataloging-in-Publication Data
Ivanhoe, P. J.
   The daodejing of laozi / translation and commentary by Philip
J. Ivanhoe.
      p. cm.
Includes bibliographical references and index.
ISBN 0-87220-701-3 (paper) 0-87220-702-1 cloth
   1. Laozi. Dao de jing. I. Laozi. Dao de jing. English. II. Title.

BL1900.L35 I93 2001
299'.51482—dc21

                                             2001005951

ISBN-13: 978-0-87220-702-8 (cloth)
ISBN-13: 978-0-87220-701-1 (pbk.)

For Qiu Qiu 球球

who "can wail all day without growing hoarse."

Contents

Preface

I have studied and loved the *Daodejing* for many years and learned a great deal about it from a wide range of teachers, colleagues, and friends and from those we must "ascend to befriend"—the classical Chinese commentators. I first undertook the translation of the text as part of the volume *Readings in Classical Chinese Philosophy* (Hackett, 2003). The version presented here is slightly different from what appears there, and this translation has more notes explaining philosophical points of interest.

I did much of the work on this manuscript during a sabbatical granted to me by the Departments of Asian Languages and Cultures and Philosophy at the University of Michigan, Ann Arbor, during the 2000–2001 academic year. I made final revisions while serving as the Austin J. Fagothy, S. J. Distinguished Visiting Professor of Philosophy at Santa Clara University, spring quarter, 2000–2001. I am most grateful to these programs and institutions for supporting my work. I would also like to thank the Center for Chinese Studies at the University of Michigan for help in preparing this volume for publication. This volume and I have both benefited greatly from the support and friendship of Jehanne Anabtawi, who has the eye of a philosopher and the heart of a poet. Special thanks to Robyn Sahleen for designing the lovely cover for this volume and to Mark Berkson, Mark Csikszentmihalyi, T.C. Kline, and Justin Tiwald for helpful suggestions on the translation and supporting material.

24 July 2003

Notes on Paintings and Calligraphy

The painting that appears on the cover of this volume is entitled *zuo kan yun qi* 坐看雲起, "Sitting, Watching Clouds Rise," by the Song dynasty painter Ma Lin 馬麟 (ca. 1180–after 1256 C.E.). It is reproduced here by permission from the Cleveland Museum of Art. Among the many virtues of this work is its ability to convey a feeling for the undifferentiated and amorphous state of being, when there was just *qi* 氣, "vital energy" and "before there were things" (see chapters 14, 21, and 25). Ma Lin also captures the sense in which the sage too attains and thereby resonates with this original state of being, keeping himself free from fixed plans and clever schemes. In this way he remains in but not wholly of the normal social world the rest of us inhabit: "I alone am still and inactive, revealing no sign" (see chapters 20, 14, and 16).

The painting that appears on the page preceding the introduction to this volume is entitled *xinglü tu* 行旅圖, "Travelers," by the Qing dynasty painter Wang Hui 王翬 (1632–1717 C.E.). It is a copy of an earlier work by the Song dynasty master Fan Kuan 范寬 (active 990–1030 C.E.) and is reproduced here by permission of the National Palace Museum, Taipei, Republic of China. This work expresses not simply a love of Nature but a sense that human beings are but one feature on the great landscape of the natural world, with no more importance than any other. Early Daoists, unlike their Confucian contemporaries, valued pristine Nature. This idea is captured in the image of "unhewn wood" that appears throughout the *Daodejing* (see chapter 15 and n. 34). This painting also captures the reverence for Nature, "the spirit of the valley," that one finds throughout the *Daodejing* (see chapter 6) and other early Daoist writings, and the special appreciation of the supple power, natural fecundity, and apparent humility of water (see chapters 8, 12, 61, 66, and 78).

The two examples of calligraphy that appear on the pages facing chapters 1 and 38 are the work of my teacher Chuang Yin 莊因. Each presents the opening lines of the chapter it precedes. (For a discussion of different translations of the first two lines of the text, see the Language Appendix to this volume.) Calligraphy is an art and a form of spiritual training practiced by educated Chinese throughout history. It is by no means an exclusively Daoist practice; however, the way in which flowing ink and soft brush can produce such powerful, vibrant, and edifying images captures a distinctively Daoist set of ideals. I am particularly honored and pleased to have these samples of my teacher's calligraphy included in this volume.

Introduction

Traditionally ascribed to the mythical Laozi 老子, who was an older contemporary of Kongzi 孔子 (Confucius), the *Laozi* or *Daodejing* 道德經 is a composite work consisting of short passages, from a variety of sources, over half of which are rhymed.[1] Different versions and fragments of the text, more or less similar to the standard text that is the basis of this translation, are extant, and there are several hundred commentaries on the *Daodejing* by Chinese, Korean, and Japanese scholars.[2] There is considerable controversy concerning the date of the text but an emerging consensus that it reached something like its present form sometime during the third century B.C.E.[3] Two versions of the text, written on silk and discovered in a tomb at *Mawangdui* 馬王堆, are firmly dated to the latter part of the second century B.C.E. In these manuscripts, the order of the books is reversed, giving us the *Dedaojing* 德道經.[4]

Much has been written about the composite nature of the *Daodejing*. However, the fact that the text draws upon multiple sources in itself does not in any way preclude the presentation of a consistent vision. Just as a cobbler can make use of various scraps of leather to fashion a very fine pair of shoes, an editor can draw upon and augment material from a variety of different sources and shape these into a coherent and elegant composition. Indeed, this process can pass through numerous iterations and through the hands of a series of different editors, generating a number of related yet equally coherent texts. Such a process may well have occurred in the case of the *Daodejing*.

The recently discovered versions of the text offer very helpful suggestions as to how to read particular lines and how one might interpret certain passages, but there is nothing in them that conflicts with or alters our understanding of the core philosophical vision of the text used by the later and highly influential commentator Wang Bi 王弼 (226–249 C.E.). I have used this version of the *Daodejing* as the basis for the present translation because unlike the recently unearthed manuscripts, which were lost to later generations of readers, the Wang Bi text has served as the standard for around two thousand years. This version of the text generated the rich commentarial tradition that is an important part of the legacy of this Daoist classic and has had the greatest and most profound influence on Chinese culture, and on Korean, Japanese, and other cultures in both premodern and contemporary times.

The Wang Bi text contains eighty-one chapters that are divided into two books. The division into two parts precedes the Wang Bi edition considerably. Later versions of the text added book and chapter titles. In the Wang Bi text, Book One consists of chapters 1 through 37, what later came to be explicitly called the *dao* 道, "Way," half of the classic, while Book Two consists of chapters 38 through 81, the *de* 德, "Virtue," half. This division does not reflect the contents of either book as a whole; however, the first chapter begins with the word *dao* and the thirty-eighth chapter begins by describing the highest *de*. Both chapters employ a kind of negative descriptive strategy, telling us what the *dao* and *de* are not. More precisely, chapter 1 seeks to disabuse us of certain common misconceptions of what the *dao* might be, while chapter 38 explains what those who possess the highest *de* do not do. This accords well with the idea that the *dao* is at some level the way things are, while *de* is the characteristic power of a creature or thing. Perhaps these stylistic similarities and the fact that together these chapters address the two

most important organizing themes in the text is what moti-
vated some later editor to choose them as the opening chapters of the two books. I have followed this traditional division of the text in the translation.

Though it was cobbled together from different sources,
many of the core sections of the *Daodejing* appear to have
been assembled during a relatively short period of time.
When it was put together, China was in the midst of a pro-
longed era of fierce interstate rivalry known as the Warring
States Period (403–221 B.C.E.). This era of Chinese history
saw the end of individual, aristocratic combat and the first
use of large armies of conscripted foot soldiers. Fortified
cities, along with their civilian populations and food sup-
plies, came to be seen as legitimate military targets. Whole
cities were sometimes put to the sword even after having
surrendered. The *Daodejing* is best understood at least in
part as a reaction to this troubled age. In it we hear the la-
ment of a time weary of war, cruelty, and chaos, one yearning
for a bygone age of innocence, security, and peace.

Wars of expansion are fiercely denounced in the text.[5]
War is represented as an evil force, a spiritual miasma born
of a ruler's insatiable desires for wealth and power (see chapters 30, 31, 46). Government corruption is also roundly con-
demned (see chapters 53, 75). Both of these complaints rest on
a common, deeper criticism of the unbounded greed and
ambition of those in power. These ideas may well have given
rise to the view that excessive desire per se is bad and the related belief that our "real" or "natural" desires are actually
quite modest and limited. The more general idea that excess
in any form is bad is poignantly captured in the image of the
"tilting vessel" of chapter 9. The text claims that it is unnatural to have excessive desires and that having them will not
only not lead to a satisfying life but will paradoxically result

in destitution, want, alienation, and self-destruction. Therefore the *Daodejing* counsels everyone, but especially those in
power, to be humble, frugal, and modest (see chapters 9, 46).

While excessive desires lead to profound misfortune,
such calamity is not regarded as an inevitable feature of the
human condition. People can pursue certain modest levels of
satisfaction without incurring any bad consequences. However, most are enticed to upset the natural balance, to embel-
lish and thereby obscure and hinder their original nature, by
pursuing excessive wealth, beauty, or power—values foisted
upon them by social conditioning. The obsessive quest to
obtain such artificial goods blinds one to the true and natural desires and leads to both physical and psychological dis-
tress (see chapters 3, 12).

Pursuing what society recommends leads one to depart
from one's authentic nature, to neglect one's "belly" in order
to please one's "eyes." Socially sanctioned notions of beauty,
music, good taste, and other sources of "satisfaction" are por-
trayed as corruptions of natural preferences. Society isolates
and exaggerates certain goods and elevates them to preemi-
nent positions of prestige. This in turn leads people to clash
and contend with one another in a mad dash to secure these
goods. The great *dao* of the Daoists eliminates the source of
such conflicts by embracing all things: the ugly as well as the
beautiful, the high as well as the low, the humble as well as
the eminent. This does not mean that for a given creature
there are not better and worse ways of being or states of affairs, only that both the good and the bad are needed in order
to maintain the greater harmony of the *dao*. For example,
while life is obviously better than death for any individual
creature, the health and well-being of the species and of the
larger biological systems of which it is but a part depend on
the fact that creatures die as well as live. Each side of dichoto-

mies such as life and death has value as part of the larger whole to which it contributes. The *Daodejing* insists that no creature can forsake its proper place and transgress its natural limits without upsetting the delicate balance of the Way. In the end, all such attempts prove not only destructive but self-defeating.

Daoists appeal to the standard of an earlier golden age in human history, before people made sharp distinctions among things. This was a time when values and qualities were not clearly distinguished, when things simply were as they were spontaneously. The next best state is when distinctions among things are made but neither side of the dichotomies that arise from such distinctions is held up as absolutely superior. The text makes a great deal of the notion that whenever one recognizes a given value or quality one brings into being the idea of its opposite as well; for example, a concept of beauty gives rise to a corresponding concept of ugliness, a notion of high brings with it a notion of low. The further claim is then made that whenever such paired concepts are sharply distinguished, there is a tendency to elevate and pursue one side while suppressing and rejecting the other. This in turn leads to an obsessive desire to possess what is favored and eliminate what is disliked. However, because of the mutual dependence of such conceptual dichotomies, this is thought to be an impossible goal, for such effort purportedly generates a contrary effect. We can imagine an example in which the pursuit of some conception of the beautiful leads one to try to eradicate all that falls short of this ideal. In such a case, beauty itself not only gives rise to but in some sense *becomes* something ugly. This is why the state before such distinctions come into being serves as the Daoist ideal. At the next stage, the best one can do is to recognize both poles of such pairs and seek a state of harmony and balance.

Many of Laozi's harshest criticisms are reserved for the ethical values of elite society. These not only are regarded as deeply hypocritical but are blamed for supporting and lending credence to the entire misguided affair of contemporary society. All such "wisdom" and "learning"— so cherished by society—is actually a horrible and corrupting influence, something people would be better off without (see chapters 19, 20, 48, 65). The rituals of the Confucians, along with their notions of benevolence, rightness, and filial piety are all debased mutations of the Natural—false and gaudy substitutes for the real things (see chapter 38).

Like most traditional Chinese thinkers, Daoists are ethical realists, though of an unusual sort. They believe that true and correct value judgments reflect objective features about the world, and they do not hesitate to criticize those who fail to accord with what is proper and fitting. Though they insist that spoken ways—that is, ways of life that can be described and codified—are incomplete and flawed, this does not entail and should not be taken as implying that they reject the idea that there is a normative *dao* for the world. The text goes to considerable lengths describing how elusive and indistinct the true *dao* is. Among other things, it is ineffable, but this does not mean either that it does not exist or that we cannot understand it.

The *Daodejing* describes a mystical ideal in the sense that those who realize the Way lose a strong sense of themselves as distinct, autonomous agents and to some extent are thought to merge into the *dao*'s underlying patterns and processes. In such a state, one does not conceive of oneself as apart from and independent of the rest of the world. While aware of herself and the things around her, such a person does not stand back to view and analyze the *dao*. Since she sees herself as inextricably intertwined with the overall harmony of the *dao*, she never assumes the perspective of a narrowly self-interested agent seeking to maximize her individual well-being. Any such higher-order perspective is alien to the Daoist ideal. The Daoist sage is guided by prereflective intuitions and tendencies rather than by preestablished or self-conscious policies or principles.

Chapter 38 describes the history of the decline of the Way from an earlier golden age to its present debased state. This decline is characterized by an increasingly rational and self-conscious picture of the world—an explicit and consistent account of the world—the antithesis of the ideal described above. The *dao* declined as civilization and high culture arose. On the level of individuals, this means that as one becomes more self-conscious of one's actions, as one reflects upon the things one does and seeks to understand why one does them, one becomes increasingly alienated from one's own true nature and the world. More and more, one comes to see oneself as cut off from and independent of the greater patterns and processes of the *dao*. And through a course of increasingly complex and abstract intellectualization, one loses touch with one's most basic sensibilities and deepest promptings. At this stage, the various virtues that are heralded as the highest achievements of civilized society become vehicles for hypocrisy, deceit, and fraud. Society represents this same phenomenon writ large.

Exactly why or how this process of alienation occurs in the first place is something the Daoists never adequately explain (and, given their views, perhaps they cannot). However, the text insists on returning to an earlier natural state when the Way was fully realized in the world. There are repeated references to "untangling," "blunting," and "rounding off" the corners of our present life. We are to let our "wheels move only along old ruts." All of these references are recommending a way of life that purportedly once was and that can be again (see chapters 40, 52, 56).[6]

Like a number of classical Chinese thinkers, early Daoists saw no essential conflict between an ethical "ought" —what is proper or fitting—and a certain sense of what naturally "is" the case. Our natural state is normative in the same way that the notion of "health" is for physical well-being. A cluster of concepts having to do with general health or human flourishing—for example, living out one's allotted span of years, keeping oneself physically whole and free from a variety of harms and deprivations, and enjoying psychological ease, comfort, and contentment—describe the core of the Daoist ideal. However, it is important to keep in mind that the natural state to which Daoists appeal is not the status quo but the *dao,* which lies beneath successive layers of socialization. For those in the fallen state of society, the *dao* is not easy to discern or to follow. The challenge is to become aware of what we—in some deep sense—are and then work to live in light of this awareness.

The *dao* is the source, sustenance, and ideal pattern for all things in the world. It is "hidden" and difficult to grasp but not metaphysically transcendent. In the apt metaphor of the text, it is the "root" of all things. The *dao* is *ziran* 自然, "so of itself" or "spontaneous," and its unencumbered activity brings about various natural states of affairs through *wuwei* 無為, "nonaction."[7] From the Daoist perspective, *ziran* is normative for states of affairs (i.e., *what* is appropriate); *wuwei* is normative for actions (i.e., *how* to act).

Human beings have a place in the *dao* but are not particularly exalted. They are simply things among things. This view is well-represented by the marvelous landscape paintings inspired by Daoism, examples of which appear on the cover and in the frontmatter of this volume.[8] Because of their unbridled desires and their unique capacity to think, act intentionally, and alter their nature—thus acting contrary to *wuwei* and bringing about states that are not *ziran*—humans tend to forsake their proper place. They attempt to set themselves above and in opposition to the natural state of affairs, that is, the *dao*. Having abandoned the natural security and contentment of the *dao*, most are led to embark upon an ever-spiraling effort to find satisfaction in increasingly unnatural and perilous pursuits, for example, the search for prestige, wealth, power, and excessive sensual stimulation. This quest proves not only futile but harmful to those driven to pursue it. Because such activity disrupts the natural harmony of the *dao*, its injurious effects spill over to harm others as well. This has been the state of things ever since human beings first fell out of the agrarian utopia of the golden age. The purpose of, or perhaps the hoped-for natural effect of reading the *Daodejing* is to undo the consequences of such misguided human views and practices and move people to "return" to the earlier ideal. The text is as much a form of philosophical or spiritual therapy as it is the presentation of a theory.[9] We are to be challenged by its paradoxes and moved by its images and poetic cadence as much as by the arguments it presents.

An appreciation of the historical context of the *Daodejing* can help us to understand its radical rejection of society and its call for a return to an earlier age of innocence, integrity, and peace. It is likely that the apparently profound disutility of innovation and achievement—its culmination in massacre, famine, hypocrisy, cruelty, and terror—moved the author or authors of the *Daodejing* to embrace the idea that the elimination of human "cleverness" and "scheming" would itself represent an improvement. Life in the much simpler, ideal Daoist world would not be perfect, human beings would still face hardships, and like the *dao* itself they would need to embrace the bad as well as the good. However, one could believe that the natural difficulties and even the natural disasters they would have to face would be less severe and debilitating than the man-made catastrophes that were becoming widespread at the time. One could see a similar widespread rejection of high culture, technology, and the intellect and a yearning for a more innocent and gentle time among North American youth in the 1960s, and one can imagine a similar frame of mind arising again in the aftermath of some future nuclear or biological holocaust or massive ecological disaster.

In order to realize the kind of life the Daoist recommends, we must pare away our inherited notions of right and wrong and return to the prereflective simplicity of Nature (see chapter 48). If people do this, society too will "return" to the earlier, golden age of the *dao*. As described in the text, this ideal age was a primitive agrarian utopia, a low-tech, highly dispersed society of independent village communities in which people found and were satisfied with simple pleasures. A ruler who wishes to bring about this happy state of affairs must dedicate himself to *undoing* the things others have worked so hard to bring about and then ensure that such pernicious ideas and practices never arise again. He must reduce the size and population of the state (see chapter 80), work to empty the people's minds and fill their bellies, weaken their wills and strengthen their bones, and then keep them innocent of knowledge and free from desire (see chapter 3). Here we see the implementation in state policy of the beliefs discussed earlier regarding what are the "real" or "natural" desires of human beings and what they need to live a contented life. The *Daodejing* assumes that what brings people the greatest overall satisfaction, what is in their true best interest, is to live an innocent agrarian life in which they are provided with basic necessities, are kept ignorant of high culture, and are free from the physical and psychological suffering that is thought to follow inevitably when "desire raises its head."

Some Chinese commentators and modern interpreters have read the *Daodejing* in a more purposive or instrumental way, that is, as a manual of various techniques that enable one to gain certain nonmoral goods such as long life, health, power, or control over others. Certain of these techniques are thought to rely on indirection, or the ability to turn an opponent's energy back upon him by employing the dynamic of "excess leading to its opposite" described above. For example, we are told that in order to weaken something, one must first strengthen it and that what is most submissive and weak can dominate the most forceful and strong (see chapters 36, 43, 61). The text also argues that the most vulnerable creatures are, when properly understood, potentially the most vital, powerful, and secure (see chapter 76).

Techniques for gaining certain nonmoral advantages can be extracted from the *Daodejing*, but when read in the context of the entire text, such purely instrumental readings appear less tenable. The *Daodejing* does claim that those who truly accord with the *dao* are protected from many common dangers and enjoy a range of enhanced abilities, benefits, and advantages. However, anyone who purposely attempts to "use" the dynamic of the *dao* to gain these or other limited, selfish goods—be they material or psychological—cannot possibly tap into its remarkable and elusive power. Anyone who tries to pursue such private, selfish aims would neither accord with the *dao* nor act with *de*, "Virtue." Hence they would utterly and completely fail to fulfill the message of the *dao*, "Way," and *de*, "Virtue," *jing*, "Classic."

Those who attempt to make use of the *dao* cannot accord with it—and hence will be undone—because they operate on consciously held and preestablished policies or principles. They step away and stand back from the great *dao* and regard other people and things as fundamentally unconnected with themselves, objects to be manipulated in their schemes of self-aggrandizement. This violates the more mystical aspects of the text, discussed above, which describe the ideal of abandoning oneself to the prereflective promptings of the *dao*, a benign and bountiful power. The great *dao* produces things without seeking to possess them and accomplishes its task without claiming credit (see chapters 2, 10, 34, 51). By following the *dao*, every thing will return to its root and proper destiny (see chapter 16). Heaven will become clear, the earth tranquil, spiritual beings divine, the valley full, and all things will flourish and grow (see chapters 32, 39).

Those who seek to manipulate the *dao* for their private advantage would also fail to generate and possess *de*, "Virtue" or "power," the personal charisma thought essential to the functioning of the entire Daoist project.[10] The Daoist sage is submissive and yielding in the sense of being open, welcoming, and nurturing. Such excellences are described in the text as distinctively female characteristics (see chapters 10, 28). The sage is like a loving mother who has unqualified and overflowing concern for all. Daoists believe that the cultivation of such dispositions not only enables one to discern and harmonize with the patterns and processes of the *dao*, it also—though unintentionally—generates *de*. *De* accrues to an individual who possesses natural calm, compassion, and confidence. It is a power thought capable of attracting, disarming, reassuring, and pacifying other people. *De* enables the sage to move others to abandon the insanity of normal society and return without coercion to the peace, contentment, and prosperity of the *dao*. *De* is even described as able to affect other creatures and inanimate objects in ways that facilitate the realization of the *dao*.[11] Anyone who tried to remove the attributes or methods of a sage from this, their full context, and employ them to achieve more limited ends or personal gain would undermine the efficacy and *de*, "power," of these teachings.

For those of us still stuck in the spiritually backward perspective of trying to "make sense" of the text, the *Daodejing* presents numerous paradoxes. One of its most pronounced and influential conundrums concerns its recommendation that we be "without desires." For those who still "have desires"—understood as meaning something like *excessive* desires—this teaching seems only to multiply their difficulties. For if they follow this advice, they then are *desiring* not to desire, simply adding fuel to their spiritually consuming fire. There is an apparent paradox to advice that counsels us to work at being relaxed or to try not to try. And those who are "without desires" are not much better off, for this teaching might well lead them to develop the prideful self-consciousness of their own goodness that elsewhere the text warns against.

However, if we understand this teaching in the greater context of the *Daodejing*, the paradox dissolves. Instead of interpreting it as an imperative to act—which leads to the difficulties described above—we should understand this teaching in more therapeutic and psychological terms, as indicating what we should be aware of and where we should focus our attention. If, as the text insists, we come to see excessive desires as debilitating and alien accretions to our true selves, this awareness alone will help loosen their grip upon us. We don't need to *do* anything in addition to gaining a sincere appreciation of their true nature. Moreover, if, as the text insists, we always have within us prereflective intuitions and tendencies that incline us to spontaneously grasp and accord with the *dao*, then by becoming aware of these and by focusing on and following them, we will be led to lose interest in and abandon our excessive desires. And we will do so without developing the debilitating delusion that we are the source of these insights. In both cases, we "do nothing yet nothing remains undone."

The paradoxical nature of the *Daodejing*, along with its poetic form, are themselves important parts of its message. The motivation for these stylistic features of the text is the belief that if we cannot reason our way out of certain problems, we can at least hope that wrestling with such paradoxes will exhaust our rational nature and loosen its grip on us. In such moments, alternative sources of insight and motivation within us, the underlying rhythms of the *dao* elicited by the enchanting and lyrical quality of the text, can slip free and supply us with understanding. However, the *Daodejing* itself tends to resist any neat attempts at analyzing its message. It refuses to fall before human "cleverness" and is careful to deny even its own authority, insisting that "Those who know do not talk [about it]; Those who talk [about it] do not know" (see chapter 56).

In arguing that human beings by nature have few basic needs and a minimum set of desires, the *Daodejing* dramatically rejects what many have taken to be our most distinctive characteristics: our intellectual abilities, our creative capacities, and our strong sense of autonomy. It tells us that these in fact are the source of some of our worst troubles. It turns out that most of life's greatest difficulties are caused by our own propensity to make our lives more complicated than they need to be. Most of the wounds we suffer are self-inflicted, and only by unlearning what we know and hold most dear can we heal ourselves. These are among the text's most dramatic claims. However, the *Daodejing* also offers more modest and equally fascinating ideas concerning moral psychology and ethical justification. In regard to the former are its insights into how a strong sense of the moral worth of one's actions not only seems to diminish their value but may in fact have a corrosive effect on one's character. A morally excellent person cannot go around announcing just how good he is. Even if such a person simply entertains too strong a sense of his own moral superiority, knowledge of this will lower others' opinion of him. One need not embrace the entire metaphysical picture or background beliefs of the *Daodejing* in order to understand and appreciate such ideas. They are perfectly comprehensible in terms of where the focus of one's motivation and attention lies. Another fascinating idea is the *Daodejing*'s distinctive conception of the cultivated person's *de*, "Virtue." The ability that certain ethically remarkable people have to attract others to them, to put them at ease, and perhaps to increase their level of self-awareness and sensitivity is a phenomenon attested in our own age as well as in this ancient classic.

In regard to ethical justification, a sense of having a place in the greater scheme of things, of finding a harmonious relationship not only between oneself and other human beings but with other creatures and things as well, might indeed be part of what defines a good life for creatures like us. If something like this view is not the case, then apart from appealing to problematic notions such as the rights of other animals, plants, and inanimate objects or the existence of nonnatural or otherwise odd moral qualities, it is hard to find any plausible justification for environmental concern, above simple prudence. We may not be able to embrace a belief in the value of a harmonious relationship with Nature in the precise sense or with the apparent certainty of early Daoists, but we may still confidently and with good reason cherish it as an important part of living well. Similarly, we need not follow all of the more dramatic claims the text makes about the need to suppress our intellect, creativity, and autonomy in order to recognize that there are inherent and distinctive dangers associated with these wonderful and characteristically human qualities. Finding a way to exercise these aspects of human nature while keeping them in their proper place might help us to protect and appreciate those prereflective and spontaneous aspects of our natures that Daoists cherish, and lead us to discover, appreciate, and live more harmonious and satisfying lives.

NOTES

1. For a discussion of the myth of Laozi, see A.C. Graham, "The Origins of the Legend of Lao Tan," and Livia Kohn, "The Lao-tzu Myth," both in Kohn and LaFargue 1998, 23–40, 41–62. The text has been referred to as a *jing* 經, "classic," since around the second or first century B.C.E.

2. For a discussion of the history of the text that explains some of the recent archeological discoveries, see the introduction in Csikszentmihalyi and Ivanhoe 1999, 1–31. For studies that concentrate on the text and commentary of Wang Bi 王弼 (226–249 C.E.), which is the text used for this translation, see Chan 1991 and Wagner 2000.

3. The most careful and complete discussion of the question of dating is the essay by William H. Baxter, "Situating the Language of the *Lao-tzu*: The Probable Date of the *Tao-te-ching*," in Kohn and LaFargue 1998, 231–53. Baxter argues for a date "around 400 B.C.E."

4. This is also the case with what is at this point the earliest known commentary on parts of the text, the *Jie Lao* 解老,

"Explaining Laozi," chapter of the *Han Feizi*. For English translations of the *Mawangdui* texts, see the Selective Bibliography.

5. This is a common theme among thinkers of this period, but in its emphasis on this theme, the *Daodejing* is similar to another influential school of thought known as Mohism. Strictly speaking, neither the Mohists nor the *Daodejing* present forms of pacifism, for they accepted and endorsed the use of force in certain situations. However, the *Daodejing* sees resorting to arms as regrettable in ways the Mohists never note. The Daoist text is much more sensitive to the physical and psychological suffering of war, especially the suffering of noncombatants. For the Mohists, see my entry on "Mohist Philosophy" in Craig 1998, 451–58.

6. While the *Daodejing* shares with such thinkers as Rousseau a favorable view of early human society and human nature, they part company on a number of issues. One such disagreement concerns our ability to work our way back to the earlier, presocial utopia. Like many Chinese texts, the *Daodejing* believes that self-cultivation can alter our present character and bring us back to an earlier, golden age. Rousseau echoes the story of the fall in *Genesis* and believes that once paradise is lost it can never be regained, at least not through human effort alone.

7. For a study of the notion of *wuwei* in early Chinese religious thought, see Slingerland (forthcoming).

8. In a fascinating and highly informative essay on Chinese landscape painting, James F. Cahill questions the claim that Daoism or Buddhism played a significant role in shaping this important movement within Chinese art. He argues that since the vast majority of painters were themselves Confucian literati and many theorists of painting used Neo-Confucian philosophical theories to explain their art, claims of Daoist or Buddhist influence are much exaggerated. While Cahill is right to insist on the importance of Confucian ideas in a wide range of aesthetic theory and endeavor, his account underestimates

the extent to which Daoist and Buddhist views of Nature and the proper relationship between self and Nature came to inform later Confucian thought and art. For example, seeing humans as but minor players on the vast stage of Nature and seeing value in untamed Nature are distinctively Daoist themes. I explore and compare Chinese views on Nature in two essays. See "Human Beings and Nature in Traditional Chinese Thought" in Deutsch and Bontekoe 1997, 155–64, and "Early Confucianism and Environmental Ethics," in Tucker and Berthrong 1998, 59–76. For Cahill's essay, see his "Confucian Elements in the Theory of Painting," in Wright 1960, 115–40.

9. The idea that philosophy is more therapeutic than theoretic is not unfamiliar to the Western tradition. For two studies that explore this aspect of philosophy, see Pierre Hadot, *Philosophy as a Way of Life*, edited and with an introduction by Arnold I. Davidson (Oxford: Blackwell, 1995), and Martha C. Nussbaum, *The Therapy of Desire: Theory and Practice in Hellenistic Ethics* (Princeton: Princeton University Press, 1994).

10. For a study of the Daoist concept of *de* that compares it with early Confucian views about the charismatic power of Virtue, see my "The Concept of *De* ("Virtue") in the *Laozi*," in Csikszentmihalyi and Ivanhoe 1999, 239–57.

11. While some of the extreme claims made on behalf of the efficacy of *de* are untenable, the idea that someone who is calm, caring, and at ease with him- or herself can affect the psychological state and physical responses of certain nonhuman creatures is not at all mysterious. Daoists can point to such nonverbal and nonpropositional communication as another example of the subtle workings of the *dao*.

Book One

道可道非常道
名可名非常名

Chapter One

A Way that can be followed is not a constant Way.[1]
A name that can be named is not a constant name.
Nameless, it is the beginning of Heaven and Earth;[2]
Named, it is the mother of the myriad creatures.
And so,

> Always eliminate desires in order to observe its
> > mysteries;
> Always have desires in order to observe its
> > manifestations.

These two come forth in unity but diverge in name.
Their unity is known as an enigma.[3]
Within this enigma is yet a deeper enigma.
The gate of all mysteries!

Chapter Two

Everyone in the world knows that when the beautiful strives
      to be beautiful, it is repulsive.
Everyone knows that when the good strives to be good, it is
      no good.[4]
And so,
    To have and to lack generate each other.[5]
    Difficult and easy give form to each other.
    Long and short off-set each other.
    High and low incline into each other.
    Note and rhythm harmonize with each other.
    Before and after follow each other.
This is why sages abide in the business of nonaction,[6]
    and practice the teaching that is without words.[7]
They work with the myriad creatures and turn none away.[8]
They produce without possessing.[9]
They act with no expectation of reward.[10]
When their work is done, they do not linger.[11]
And, by not lingering, merit never deserts them.

Chapter Three

Not paying honor to the worthy leads the people to avoid
        contention.

Not showing reverence for precious goods leads them to not
        steal.[12]

Not making a display of what is desirable leads their hearts
        away from chaos.[13]

This is why sages bring things to order by opening people's
        hearts[14]

    and filling their bellies.

They weaken the people's commitments and strengthen
        their bones;

They make sure that the people are without knowledge or
        desires;

And that those with knowledge do not dare to act.

Sages enact nonaction and everything becomes well ordered.

Chapter Four

The Way is like an empty vessel;
No use could ever fill it up.
Vast and deep!
It seems to be the ancestor of the myriad creatures.
It blunts their sharpness;[15]
Untangles their tangles;
Softens their glare;
Merges with their dust.
Deep and clear!
It seems to be there.
I do not know whose child it is;
It is the image of what was before the Supreme Spirit
          himself![16]

Chapter Five

Heaven and Earth are not benevolent;
They treat the myriad creatures as straw dogs.[17]
Sages are not benevolent;
They treat the people as straw dogs.
Is not the space between Heaven and Earth like a bellows?
Empty yet inexhaustible!
Work it and more will come forth.
An excess of speech will lead to exhaustion,[18]
It is better to hold on to the mean.

Chapter Six

The spirit of the valley never dies;
She is called the Enigmatic Female.
The portal of the Enigmatic Female;
Is called the root of Heaven and Earth.
An unbroken, gossamer thread;
It seems to be there.
But use will not unsettle it.

Chapter Seven

Heaven is long lasting;
Earth endures.
Heaven is able to be long lasting and Earth is able to endure,
    because they do not live for themselves.
And so, they are able to be long lasting and to endure.
This is why sages put themselves last and yet come first;
Treat themselves as unimportant and yet are preserved.
Is it not because they have no thought of themselves, that they
        are able to perfect themselves?

Chapter Eight

The highest good is like water.
Water is good at benefiting the myriad creatures, while not
        contending with them.
It resides in places that people find repellent, and so comes
        close to the Way.
    In a residence, the good lies in location.
    In hearts, the good lies in depth.
    In interactions with others, the good lies in
        benevolence.
    In words, the good lies in trustworthiness.
    In government, the good lies in orderliness.
    In carrying out one's business, the good lies in ability.
    In actions, the good lies in timeliness.[19]
Only by avoiding contention can one avoid blame.

Chapter Nine

To hold the vessel upright in order to fill it is not as good as
      to stop in time.[20]
If you make your blade too keen it will not hold its edge.
When gold and jade fill the hall none can hold on to them.
To be haughty when wealth and honor come your way is to
      bring disaster upon yourself.
To withdraw when the work is done is the Way of Heaven.[21]

Chapter Ten

Embracing your soul and holding on to the One, can you
keep them from departing?[22]
Concentrating your *qi* ("vital energies") and attaining the
utmost suppleness,
can you be a child?[23]
Cleaning and purifying your enigmatic vision, can you be
without flaw?[24]
Caring for the people and ordering the state, can you
eliminate all knowledge?
When the portal of Heaven opens and closes, can you play
the part of the feminine?
Comprehending all within the four directions, can you
reside in nonaction?
To produce them!
To nurture them!
To produce without possessing;[25]
To act with no expectation of reward;[26]
To lead without lording over;
Such is Enigmatic Virtue![27]

Chapter Eleven

Thirty spokes are joined in the hub of a wheel.
But only by relying on what is not there, do we have the use
      of the carriage.[28]
By adding and removing clay we form a vessel.
But only by relying on what is not there, do we have use of
      the vessel.
By carving out doors and windows we make a room.
But only by relying on what is not there, do we have use of
      the room.
And so, what is there is the basis for profit;
What is not there is the basis for use.

Chapter Twelve

The five colors blind our eyes.[29]
The five notes deafen our ears.
The five flavors deaden our palates.
The chase and the hunt madden our hearts.
Precious goods impede our activities.
This is why sages are for the belly and not for the eye;
And so they cast off the one and take up the other.[30]

Chapter Thirteen

Be apprehensive about favor or disgrace.
Revere calamity as you revere your own body.
What does it mean to be apprehensive about favor and
disgrace?
To receive favor is to be in the position of a subordinate.
When you get it be apprehensive;
When you lose it be apprehensive.
This is what it means to be apprehensive about favor and
disgrace.
What does it mean to revere calamity as you revere your own
body?
I can suffer calamity only because I have a body.
When I no longer have a body, what calamity could I
possibly have?
And so,
Those who revere their bodies as if they were the entire
world
can be given custody of the world.
Those who care for their bodies as if they were the
entire world
can be entrusted with the world.

Chapter Fourteen

Looked for but not seen, its name is "miniscule."
Listened for but not heard, its name is "rarified."
Grabbed for but not gotten, its name is "subtle."[31]
These three cannot be perfectly explained, and so are
        confused and regarded as one.
Its top is not clear or bright,
Its bottom is not obscure or dark.
Trailing off without end, it cannot be named.
It returns to its home, back before there were things.[32]
This is called the formless form, the image of no thing.[33]
This is called the confused and indistinct.
Greet it and you will not see its head;
Follow it and you will not see its tail.
Hold fast to the Way of old, in order to control what is here
        today.
The ability to know the ancient beginnings, this is called the
        thread of the Way.

Chapter Fifteen

In ancient times, the best and most accomplished scholars
Were subtle, mysterious, enigmatic, and far-reaching.
Their profundity was beyond understanding.
Because they were beyond understanding, only with
        difficulty can we try to describe them:
    Poised, like one who must ford a stream in winter.
    Cautious, like one who fears his neighbors on every side.
    Reserved, like a visitor.
    Opening up, like ice about to break.
    Honest, like unhewn wood.[34]
    Broad, like a valley.
    Turbid, like muddy water.
Who can, through stillness, gradually make muddied water
        clear?
Who can, through movement, gradually stir to life what has
        long been still?
Those who preserve this Way do not desire fullness.
And, because they are not full, they have no need for renewal.

Chapter Sixteen

Attain extreme tenuousness;
Preserve quiet integrity.
The myriad creatures are all in motion!
I watch as they turn back.[35]
The teeming multitude of things, each returns home to its
        root;
And returning to one's root is called stillness.
This is known as returning to one's destiny;
And returning to one's destiny is known as constancy.
To know constancy is called "enlightenment."
Those who do not know constancy wantonly produce
        misfortune.
To know constancy is to be accommodating.
To be accommodating is to work for the good of all.
To work for the good of all is to be a true king.
To be a true king is to be Heavenly.
To be Heavenly is to embody the Way.
To embody the Way is to be long lived,
And one will avoid danger to the end of one's days.[36]

Chapter Seventeen

The greatest of rulers is but a shadowy presence;
Next is the ruler who is loved and praised;
Next is the one who is feared;
Next is the one who is reviled.
Those lacking in trust are not trusted.[37]
However, [the greatest rulers] are cautious and honor
        words.[38]
When their task is done and work complete,[39]
Their people all say, "This is just how we are."[40]

Chapter Eighteen

When the great Way is abandoned, there are benevolence
and righteousness.
When wisdom and intelligence come forth, there is great
hypocrisy.
When the six familial relationships are out of balance, there
are kind parents and filial children.
When the state is in turmoil and chaos, there are loyal
ministers.[41]

Chapter Nineteen

Cut off sageliness, abandon wisdom, and the people will
         benefit one hundred fold.
Cut off benevolence, abandon righteousness, and the people
         will return to being filial and kind.
Cut off cleverness, abandon profit, and robbers and thieves
         will be no more.
This might leave the people lacking in culture;
So give them something with which to identify:
    Manifest plainness.
    Embrace simplicity.[42]
    Do not think just of yourself.
    Make few your desires.

Chapter Twenty

Cut off learning and be without worry!
How much distance is there between agreement and
                flattery?
How much difference is there between the fair and the foul?
What other people fear one cannot but fear.[43]
        Immense!
        Yet still not at its limit!
The multitude are bright and merry;
As if enjoying a grand festival;
As if ascending a terrace in springtime.
I alone am still and inactive, revealing no sign;[44]
Like a child who has not yet learned to smile.
Weak and weary, I seem to have nowhere to go.
The multitude all have more than enough.
I alone seem to be at a loss.
        I have the mind of a fool!
        Listless and blank!
The common folk are bright and brilliant.
I alone am muddled and confused.
The common folk are careful and discriminating.
I alone am dull and inattentive.
        Vast!
        Like the ocean!
        Blown about!
        As if it would never end!
The multitude all have something to do.
I alone remain obstinate and immobile, like some old rustic.
I alone differ from others, and value being nourished by
                mother.

Chapter Twenty-one

The outward appearance of great Virtue comes forth from
the Way alone.
As for the Way, it is vague and elusive.

Vague and elusive!
Within is an image.[45]
Vague and elusive!
Within is a thing.
Withdrawn and dark!
Within is an essence.
This essence is genuine and authentic.
Within there is trust.

From ancient times until the present day, its name has never
forsaken it.
It is how we know the origin of all things.
How do I know what the origin of all things is like?
Through this!

Chapter Twenty-two

Those who are crooked will be perfected.
Those who are bent will be straight.
Those who are empty will be full.
Those who are worn will be renewed.
Those who have little will gain.
Those who have plenty will be confounded.

This is why sages embrace the One and serve as models for
the whole world.[46]

> They do not make a display of themselves and so are
> illustrious.
> They do not affirm their own views and so are well
> known.
> They do not brag about themselves and so are accorded
> merit.
> They do not boast about themselves and so are heard of
> for a long time.[47]

Because they do not contend, no one in the world can
contend with them.[48]
The ancient saying, "Those who are crooked will be
perfected," is not without substance![49]
Truly the sages are and remain perfect.

Chapter Twenty-three

To be sparing with words is what comes naturally.
And so,
> A blustery wind does not last all morning;
> A heavy downpour does not last all day.
Who produces these?
Heaven and Earth!
If not even Heaven and Earth can keep things going for a
> long time,
How much less can human beings?
This is why one should follow the Way in all that one does.
One who follows the Way identifies with the Way.
One who follows Virtue identifies with Virtue.
One who follows loss identifies with loss.
The Way is pleased to have those who identify with the Way.
Virtue is pleased to have those who identify with Virtue.
Loss is pleased to have those who identify with loss.
Those lacking in trust are not trusted.[50]

Chapter Twenty-four

Those who stand on tiptoe cannot stand firm.
Those who stride cannot go far.

> Those who make a display of themselves are not
> illustrious.

> Those who affirm their own views are not well-known.

> Those who brag about themselves are not accorded
> merit.

> Those who boast about themselves are not heard of for
> long.[51]

From the point of view of the Way, such things are known as
"excess provisions and pointless activities."

All creatures find these repulsive;

And so one who has the Way does not abide in them.[52]

Chapter Twenty-five

There is a thing confused yet perfect, which arose before
　　　　Heaven and Earth.
Still and indistinct, it stands alone and unchanging.
It goes everywhere and is never at a loss.
One can regard it as the mother of Heaven and Earth.
I do not know its proper name;
I have styled it "the Way."[53]
Forced to give it a proper name, I would call it "Great."
The Great passes on;
What passes on extends into the distance;
What passes into the distance returns to its source.[54]
And so the Way is great;
Heaven is great;
Earth is great;
And a true king too is great.
In the universe are four things that are great and the true
　　　　king is first among them.
People model themselves on the Earth.
The Earth models itself on Heaven.
Heaven models itself on the Way.
The Way models itself on what is natural.[55]

Chapter Twenty-six

The heavy is the root of the light.
The still rules over the agitated.[56]
This is why sages travel all day without leaving their baggage
    wagons.
No matter how magnificent the view or lovely the place,
    they remain aloof and unaffected.
How can a lord who can field ten thousand chariots take
    lightly his role in the world!
If he is light, he loses the root;
If he is agitated, he loses his rule.

Chapter Twenty-seven

Those good at traveling leave no tracks or traces.
Those good at speaking are free of slips or flaws.
Those good at numbers need not count or reckon.
Those good at closing up need no bolts or locks,
    yet what they have secured cannot be opened.
Those good at binding need no rope or string,
    yet what they have tied cannot be undone.
This is why sages are good at saving people and so never
        abandon people,[57]
Are good at saving things and so never abandon things.
This is called inheriting enlightenment.[58]
And so the good person is teacher of the bad;
The bad person is material for the good.
Those who do not honor their teachers or who fail to care
        for their material,
    though knowledgeable are profoundly deluded.
This is a fundamental mystery.

Chapter Twenty-eight

Know the male but preserve the female, and be a canyon for
      all the world.
If you are a canyon for all the world, constant Virtue will
      never leave you,
    and you can return home to be a child.
Know the white but preserve the black, and be a model for
      all the world.
If you are a model for all the world, constant Virtue will
      never err,
    and you can return home to the infinite.
Know glory but preserve disgrace, and be a valley for all the
      world.
If you are a valley for all the world, constant Virtue will
      always be sufficient,
    and you can return to being unhewn wood.[59]
When unhewn wood is broken up, it becomes vessels.[60]
Sages put these to use and become leaders of the officials.
And so the greatest carving cuts nothing off.

Chapter Twenty-nine

Those who would gain the world and do something with it,
            I see that they will fail.[61]
For the world is a spiritual vessel and one cannot put it to
            use.
      Those who use it ruin it.
      Those who grab hold of it lose it.[62]

And so,
      Sometimes things lead and sometimes they follow;
      Sometimes they breathe gently and sometimes they pant;
      Sometimes they are strong and sometimes they are
            weak;
      Sometimes they fight and sometimes they fall;

This is why sages cast off whatever is extreme, extravagant,
            or excessive.

Chapter Thirty

Those who serve their ruler with the Way will never take the
     world by force of arms.
For such actions tend to come back in kind.
Wherever an army resides, thorns and thistles grow.
In the wake of a large campaign, bad harvests are sure to
     follow.
Those who are good at military action achieve their goal and
     then stop.
They do not dare rely on force of arms.
They achieve their goal but do not brag.
They achieve their goal but do not boast.
They achieve their goal but are not arrogant.
They achieve their goal but only because they have no choice.
They achieve their goal but do not force the issue.
For after a period of vigor there is old age.
To rely on such practices is said to be contrary to the Way.
And what is contrary to the Way will come to an early end.[63]

Chapter Thirty-one

Fine weapons are inauspicious instruments;
All creatures find them repulsive.
And so one who has the Way does not rely upon them.
At home, a cultivated person gives precedence to the left;
At war, a cultivated person gives precedence to the right.[64]
Weapons are inauspicious instruments, not the instruments
        of a cultivated person.
But if given no choice, the cultivated person will use them.
Peace and quiet are the highest ideals;
A military victory is not a thing of beauty.
To beautify victory is to delight in the slaughter of human
        beings.
One who delights in the slaughter of human beings will not
        realize his ambitions in the world.
On auspicious occasions, precedence is given to the left;
On inauspicious occasions, precedence is given to the right.
The lieutenant commander is stationed on the left;
The supreme commander is stationed on the right.
This shows that the supreme commander is associated with
        the rites of mourning.
When great numbers of people have been killed, one weeps
        for them in grief and sorrow.
Military victory is thus associated with the rites of
        mourning.

Chapter Thirty-two

The Way is forever nameless.[65]
Unhewn wood[66] is insignificant, yet no one in the world can
        master it.
If barons and kings could preserve it, the myriad creatures
        would all
    defer to them of their own accord;
Heaven and Earth would unite and sweet dew would fall;
The people would be peaceful and just, though no one so
        decrees.
When unhewn wood is carved up, then there are names.
Now that there are names, know enough to stop!
To know when to stop is how to stay out of danger.[67]
Streams and torrents flow into rivers and oceans,
Just as the world flows into the Way.

Chapter Thirty-three

Those who know others are knowledgeable;
Those who know themselves are enlightened.
Those who conquer others have power;
Those who conquer themselves are strong.
Those who know contentment are rich.[68]
Those who persevere have firm commitments.
Those who do not lose their place will endure.
Those who die a natural death are long-lived.[69]

Chapter Thirty-four

How expansive is the great Way!
Flowing to the left and to the right.
The myriad creatures rely upon it for life, and it turns none
      of them away.[70]
When its work is done it claims no merit.[71]
It clothes and nourishes the myriad creatures, but does not
      lord it over them.
Because it is always without desires, one could consider it
      insignificant.[72]
Because the myriad creatures all turn to it and yet it does not
      lord it over them,
   one could consider it great.
Because it never considers itself great, it is able to perfect its
      greatness.

Chapter Thirty-five

Hold on to the great image and the whole world will come
to you.[73]
They will come and suffer no harm;
They will be peaceful, secure, and prosperous.
Music and fine food will induce the passer-by to stop.
But talk about the Way—how insipid and without relish it
is!
Look for it and it cannot be seen;
Listen for it and it cannot be heard;
But use it and it will never run dry!

Chapter Thirty-six

What you intend to shrink, you first must stretch.
What you intend to weaken, you first must strengthen.
What you intend to abandon, you first must make flourish.
What you intend to steal from, you first must provide for.
This is called subtle enlightenment.
The supple and weak overcome the hard and the strong.
Fish should not be taken out of the deep pools.
The sharp implements of the state should not be shown to
         the people.[74]

Chapter Thirty-seven

The Way does nothing yet nothing is left undone.[75]
Should barons and kings be able to preserve it,
    the myriad creatures will transform themselves.[76]
After they are transformed, should some still desire to act,
I shall press them down with the weight of nameless unhewn
        wood.[77]
Nameless unhewn wood is but freedom from desire.
Without desire and still, the world will settle itself.

Book Two

上德不德是以有德

下德不失德是以無德

Chapter Thirty-eight

Those of highest Virtue do not strive for Virtue and so they
        have it.
Those of lowest Virtue never stray from Virtue and so they
        lack it.
Those of highest Virtue practice nonaction and never act for
        ulterior motives.
Those of lowest Virtue act and always have some ulterior
        motive.
Those of highest benevolence act, but without ulterior
        motives.
Those of highest righteousness act, but with ulterior
        motives.
Those who are ritually correct act, but if others do not
        respond,
    they roll up their sleeves and resort to force.[78]
And so,
    When the Way was lost there was Virtue;
    When Virtue was lost there was benevolence;
    When benevolence was lost there was righteousness;
    When righteousness was lost there were the rites.
The rites are the wearing thin of loyalty and trust, and the
        beginning of chaos.
The ability to predict what is to come is an embellishment of
        the Way,
    and the beginning of ignorance.
This is why the most accomplished reside in what is thick,
        not in what is thin.
They reside in what is most substantial, not in mere
        embellishment.
And so they cast off the one and take up the other.[79]

Chapter Thirty-nine

In the past, among those who attained the One were these:[80]
 Heaven attained the One and became pure;
 Earth attained the One and became settled;
 The spirits attained the One and became numinous;
 The valley attained the One and became full;
 The myriad creatures attained the One and flourished;
 Barons and kings attained the One and became
  mainstays of the state.
All of this came about through the One.
If Heaven lacked what made it pure, it might rip apart.
If Earth lacked what made it settled it might open up.
If the spirits lacked what made them numinous they might
  cease their activity.
If the valley lacked what made it full it might run dry.
If the myriad creatures lacked what made them flourish they
  might become extinct.
If barons and kings lacked what made them honored and
  lofty they might fall.
And so what is honored has its root in what is base;
What is lofty has its foundation in what is lowly.
This is why barons and kings refer to themselves as
 "The Orphan," "The Desolate," or "The Forlorn."[81]
Is this not a case where what is base serves as the foundation!
Is it not?
And so the greatest of praise is without praise.
Do not desire what jingles like jade,
  but what rumbles like rock!

Chapter Forty

Turning back is how the Way moves.
Weakness is how the Way operates.
The world and all its creatures arise from what is there;
What is there arises from what is not there.

Chapter Forty-one

When the best scholars hear about the Way,
They assiduously put it into practice.
When average scholars hear about the Way,
They sometimes uphold it and sometimes forsake it.
When the worst scholars hear about the Way,
They laugh at it!
If they did not laugh at it, it would not really be the Way.
And so the common saying has it:

> The clearest Way seems obscure;
> The Way ahead seems to lead backward;
> The most level Way seems uneven;
> Highest Virtue seems like a valley;
> Great purity seems sullied,
> Ample Virtue seems insufficient;
> Solid Virtue seems unstable;
> The simple and genuine seems fickle;
> The great square has no corners;
> The great vessel takes long to perfect;
> The great note sounds faint;
> The great image is without shape.[82]
> The Way is hidden and without name.[83]

Only the Way is good at providing and completing.

Chapter Forty-two

The Way produces the One.
The One produces two.
Two produces three.
Three produces the myriad creatures.[84]
The myriad creatures shoulder *yin* and embrace *yang*,
    and by blending these *qi* ("vital energies") they attain
        harmony.
People most despise being orphaned, desolate, or forlorn,
    and yet barons and kings take these as their personal
        appellations.[85]
And so sometimes diminishing a thing adds to it;
Sometimes adding to a thing diminishes it.
What others teach, I too teach: "The violent and overbearing
        will not die a natural death."
I shall take this as the father of all my teachings.

Chapter Forty-three

The most supple things in the world ride roughshod over
      the most rigid.
That which is not there can enter in, even where there is no
      space.
This is how I know the advantages of nonaction!
The teaching that is without words,[86]
The advantages of nonaction,
Few in the world attain these.

Chapter Forty-four

Your name or your body, which do you hold more dear?
Your body or your property, which is of greater value?
Gain or loss, which is the greater calamity?
For this reason, deep affections give rise to great
        expenditures.
Excessive hoarding results in great loss.
Know contentment and avoid disgrace;[87]
Know when to stop and avoid danger;[88]
And you will long endure.

Chapter Forty-five

Great perfection seems wanting but use will not wear it out.
Great fullness seems empty but use will not drain it.
Great straightness seems crooked;
Great skillfulness seems clumsy;
Great speech seems to stammer.
Agitation overcomes cold.
Stillness overcomes heat.
Purity and stillness rectify Heaven and Earth.

Chapter Forty-six

When the world has the Way, fleet-footed horses are used to
      haul dung.
When the world is without the Way, war horses are raised in
      the suburbs.[89]
The greatest misfortune is not to know contentment.[90]
The worst calamity is the desire to acquire.
And so those who know the contentment of contentment are
      always content.[91]

Chapter Forty-seven

Without going out the door, one can know the whole world.
Without looking out the window, one can see the Way of
　　　　　Heaven.
The farther one goes, the less one knows.
This is why sages
　　　Know without going abroad,
　　　Name without having to see,
　　　Perfect through nonaction.

Chapter Forty-eight

In the pursuit of learning, one does more each day;
In the pursuit of the Way, one does less each day;
One does less and less until one does nothing;[92]
One does nothing yet nothing is left undone.[93]
Gaining the world always is accomplished by following no
activity.[94]
As soon as one actively tries, one will fall short of gaining the
world.

Chapter Forty-nine

Sages do not have constant hearts of their own;
They take the people's hearts as their hearts.

    I am good to those who are good;

    I also am good to those who are not good;

    This is to be good out of Virtue.[95]

    I trust the trustworthy;

    I also trust the untrustworthy.

    This is to trust out of Virtue.

Sages blend into the world and accord with the people's
       hearts.

The people all pay attention to their eyes and ears;
The sages regard them as children.

Chapter Fifty

Between life and death,
Three out of ten are the disciples of life;[96]
Three out of ten are the disciples of death;
Three out of ten create a place for death.[97]
Why is this?
Because of their profound desire to live.[98]
I have heard that those good at nurturing life,
On land do not meet with rhinoceroses or tigers,
And in battle do not encounter armored warriors.
Rhinoceroses find no place to thrust their horns;
Tigers find no place to sink their claws;
Soldiers find no place to drive in their blades.
Why is this?
Because such people have no place for death.

Chapter Fifty-one

The Way produces them;
Virtue rears them;
Things shape them;
Circumstances perfect them.
This is why the myriad creatures all revere the Way and
        honor Virtue.
The Way is revered and Virtue honored not because this is
       decreed,
    but because it is natural.
And so the Way produces them and Virtue rears them;
    Raises and nurtures them;
    Settles and confirms them;
    Nourishes and shelters them.
To produce without possessing;[99]
To act with no expectation of reward;[100]
To lead without lording over;
Such is Enigmatic Virtue![101]

Chapter Fifty-two

The world had a beginning;
This can be considered the mother of the world.
Knowing the mother, return and know her children;
Knowing her children, return and preserve their mother;
And you will avoid danger to the end of your days.[102]
Stop up the openings;
Close the gates;[103]
To the end of your life you will remain unperturbed.
Unstop the openings;
Multiply your activities;
And to the end of your life you will be beyond salvation.
To discern what is small is called "enlightenment."
To preserve what is weak is called "strength."
Use this light and return home to this enlightenment.
Do not bring disaster upon yourself.
This is called "practicing the constant."

Chapter Fifty-three

If I know anything at all, it is that in following the great
       Way, there is but one concern:
    The great Way is smooth and easy;
    Yet people love to take shortcuts![104]
The court is resplendent;
Yet the fields are overgrown.
The granaries are empty;
Yet some wear elegant clothes;
Fine swords dangle at their sides;
They are stuffed with food and drink;
And possess wealth in gross abundance.
This is known as taking pride in robbery.
Far is this from the Way!

Chapter Fifty-four

What is firmly embedded will not be pulled out.
What is firmly embraced will not be lost.
Through the sacrifices of one's descendants, it will never
cease.
Cultivate it in oneself and its Virtue will be genuine.[105]
Cultivate it in one's family and its Virtue will be more than
enough.
Cultivate it in one's village and its Virtue will be long-
lasting.
Cultivate it in one's state and its Virtue will be abundant.
Cultivate it throughout the world and its Virtue will be
everywhere.[106]
And so, take stock of the self by looking at the self;
Take stock of the family by looking at the family;
Take stock of the village by looking at the village;
Take stock of the state by looking at the state;
Take stock of the world by looking at the world;
How do I know that the world is this way?
Through this!

Chapter Fifty-five

Those who are steeped in Virtue are like newborn
　　　　children;[107]
Poisonous creatures will not strike them;
Fierce beasts will not seize them;
Birds of prey will not snatch them away.
Their bones are weak and sinews yielding and yet their grip
　　　　is firm.
They do not yet know the union of male and female, but
　　　　their potency is at its height.
This is because they are perfectly pure;
They can wail all day without growing hoarse.
This is because they are perfectly balanced.
Knowing balance is called "constancy."
Knowing constancy is called "enlightenment."
What helps life along is called "inauspicious."[108]
When the heart–and–mind is used to guide the vital
　　　　energies, this is called "forcing things."[109]
For after a period of vigor there is old age.
To rely on such practices is said to be contrary to the Way.
And what is contrary to the Way will come to an early end.[110]

Chapter Fifty-six

Those who know do not talk [about it];
Those who talk [about it] do not know.[111]
Stop up the openings;
Close the gates;[112]
Blunt the sharpness;
Untangle the tangles;
Soften the glare;
Merge with the dust.[113]
This is known as Enigmatic Unity.[114]
And so one can neither be too familiar with nor too distant
      from them;
One can neither benefit nor harm them;
One can neither honor nor demean them,
And so they are honored by the whole world.[115]

Chapter Fifty-seven

Follow what is correct and regular in ordering your state;
Follow what is strange and perverse in deploying your
        troops;
Follow no activity and gain the world.[116]
How do I know that things are this way?
Through this!
The more taboos and prohibitions there are in the world,
        the poorer the people.
The more sharp implements the people have, the more
        benighted the state.[117]
The more clever and skillful the people, the more strange
        and perverse things arise.
The more clear the laws and edicts, the more thieves and
        robbers.
And so sages say,
      "I do nothing and the people transform themselves;[118]
      I prefer stillness and the people correct and regulate
        themselves;
      I engage in no activity and the people prosper on their
        own;
      I am without desires and the people simplify[119] their
        own lives."

Chapter Fifty-eight

The more dull and dispirited the government, the more
       honest and agreeable the people.
The more active and searching the government, the more
       deformed and deficient the people.
Good fortune rests upon disaster;
Disaster lies hidden within good fortune.
Who knows the highest standards?
Perhaps there is nothing that is truly correct and regular!
What is correct and regular turns strange and perverse;
What is good turns monstrous.
Long indeed have the people been deluded.
And so sages are,

    Square but do not cut,
    Cornered but do not clip,
    Upright but not imposing,
    Shining but not dazzling.

Chapter Fifty-nine

In bringing order to the people or in serving Heaven,
        nothing is as good as frugality.
To be frugal is called submitting early on.
Submitting early on is known as deeply accumulating
        Virtue.
If you deeply accumulate Virtue, nothing can stand in your
        way.
If nothing can stand in your way, no one will know your
        limits.
If no one knows your limits, you can possess the state.
If you possess the mother of the state, you can long endure.
This is known as deep roots and strong stems.
This is the Way of long life and far-reaching vision.

Chapter Sixty

Ruling a great state is like cooking a small fish.[120]
When one manages the world through the Way, ghosts lose
       their numinous qualities.
It's not that ghosts really lose their numinous qualities,
    but that their numinous qualities do not injure human
       beings.[121]
Not only do their numinous qualities not injure human
       beings,
    sages too do not injure human beings.[122]
Since neither of these two injures human beings, Virtue
       gathers and accrues to both.

Chapter Sixty-one

A great state is like the delta of a mighty river;[123]
It is where the whole world gathers.
It is the female of the whole world.[124]
The female always gets the better of the male through
       stillness.
Through stillness, she places herself below the male.
And so, a great state, by placing itself below a lesser state, can
       take the lesser state.
A lesser state, by placing itself below a great state, can be
       taken by the greater state.
And so, one places itself below in order to take;
The other places itself below in order to be taken.
The great state wants no more than to provide for all people
       alike.
The lesser state wants no more than to find someone to serve.
Since both can get what they want, it is fitting that the great
       state place itself in the lower position.

Chapter Sixty-two

The Way is the inner sanctum of the myriad creatures.[125]
It is the treasure of the good man and the savior of the bad.
Fine words can sell things;[126]
Noble deeds can promote someone;
But can one cast away the bad in people?[127]
And so, when setting up the Son of Heaven or appointing the
        Three Ministers,[128]
Those who offer up precious jades and present fine steeds are
        not as good
    as those who stay in their seats and promote this Way.
Why was this Way so honored in ancient times?
Did they not say that through it,
    "One could get what one seeks and escape punishment
        for one's crimes?"
And so, this is why it is honored by the whole world.[129]

Chapter Sixty-three

Act, but through nonaction.
Be active, but have no activities.[130]
Taste, but have no tastes.[131]
No matter how great or small, many or few,
Repay resentment with Virtue.[132]
Plan for what is difficult while it is easy.
Work at what is great while it is small.
The difficult undertakings in the world all start with what is
    easy.
The great undertakings in the world all begin with what is
    small.
This is why sages never work at great things and are able to
    achieve greatness.
Those who easily enter into promises always prove unworthy
    of trust.
Those who often think that things are easy regularly
    encounter difficulties.
And so sages consider things difficult and in the end are
    without difficulties.

Chapter Sixty-four

What is at peace is easy to secure.
What has yet to begin is easy to plan for.
What is brittle is easy to scatter.
What is faint is easy to disperse.
Work at things before they come to be;
Regulate things before they become disordered.
A tree whose girth fills one's embrace sprang from a downy
        sprout;
A terrace nine stories high arose from a layer of dirt;
A journey of a thousand leagues began with a single step.
    Those who use it ruin it.
    Those who grab hold of it lose it.[133]
This is why sages practice nonaction and so do not ruin;
They do not lay hold and so do not lose.
People often ruin things just when they are on the verge of
        success.
Be as careful at the end as you are at the beginning and you
        will not ruin things.
This is why sages desire to be without desires and show no
        regard for precious goods.[134]
They study what is not studied and return to what the
        multitude pass by.[135]
They work to support the myriad creatures in their natural
        condition and never dare to act.

Chapter Sixty-five

In ancient times, those good at practicing the Way did not
        use it to enlighten the people,
    but rather to keep them in the dark.[136]
The people are hard to govern because they know too much.
And so to rule a state with knowledge is to be a detriment to
        the state.
Not to rule a state through knowledge is to be a blessing to
        the state.
Know that these two provide the standard.
Always to know this standard is called Enigmatic Virtue.[137]
How profound and far-reaching is Enigmatic Virtue!
It turns back with things;
And only then is there the Great Compliance.[138]

Chapter Sixty-six

The rivers and ocean are able to rule over a hundred valleys,
    because they are good at placing themselves in the lower
        position.[139]
And so they are able to rule over a hundred valleys.
This is why if you want to be above the people you must
        proclaim that you are below them.
If you want to lead the people, you must put yourself behind
        them.
This is how sages are able to reside above the people without
        being considered a burden,
How they are able to be out in front of the people without
        being regarded as a harm.
This is why the whole world delights in supporting them
        and never wearies.
Because they do not contend, no one in the world can
        contend with them.[140]

Chapter Sixty-seven

The whole world agrees in saying that my Way is great but
        appears unworthy.
It is only because it is great that it appears to be unworthy.
If it appeared worthy, it would have become small long ago.
Isn't that so!
I have three treasures that I hold on to and preserve:
        The first I call loving-kindness;
        The second I call frugality;
        The third I call never daring to put oneself first in the
        world.
The kind can be courageous;
The frugal can be generous;
Those who never dare to put themselves first in the world
        can become leaders of the various officials.
Now to be courageous without loving-kindness,
To be generous without frugality,
To put oneself first without putting oneself behind others,
These will lead to death.[141]
If one has loving-kindness, in attack one will be victorious,
In defense one will be secure.
For Heaven will save you and protect you with loving-
        kindness.

Chapter Sixty-eight

Those good at fighting are never warlike.[142]
Those good at attack are never enraged.
Those good at conquering their enemies never confront
them.
Those good at using others put themselves in a lower
position.
This is called the Virtue of noncontention;
This is called the power of using others;
This is called matching up with Heaven, the highest
achievement of the ancients.

Chapter Sixty-nine

Military strategists have a saying,
>"I never dare to play host but prefer to play guest.[143]
>I never dare to advance an inch but retreat a foot."
This is called a formation without form,
Rolling up one's sleeve but having no arm,
Forcing the issue but lacking an enemy.[144]
Who can avoid misfortune in war?
But there is none greater than underestimating the enemy!
Underestimating the enemy almost cost me my three
>treasures.[145]
And so when swords are crossed and troops clash, the side
>that grieves shall be victorious.

Chapter Seventy

My teachings are easy to understand and easy to
    implement;[146]
But no one in the whole world has been able to understand
    or implement them.
My teachings have an ancestor and my activities have a lord;
But people fail to understand these and so I am not
    understood.
Those who understand me are rare;[147]
Those who take me as a model are honored.
This is why sages wear coarse cloth while cherishing
    precious jade.[148]

Chapter Seventy-one

To know that one does not know is best;
Not to know but to believe that one knows is a disease.[149]
Only by seeing this disease as a disease can one be free of it.
Sages are free of this disease;
Because they see this disease as a disease, they are free of it.

Chapter Seventy-two

When the people do not fear what warrants awe,
Something truly awful will come to them.
Do not constrain their homes or villages.
Do not oppress their lives.
Because you do not oppress them, you will not be oppressed.
This is why sages know themselves but do not make a display
     of themselves;
They care for themselves but do not revere themselves.
And so they cast off the one and take up the other.[150]

Chapter Seventy-three

To be courageous in daring leads to death;
To be courageous in not daring leads to life.
These two bring benefit to some and loss to others.
Who knows why Heaven dislikes what it does?
Even sages regard this as a difficult question.
The Way does not contend but is good at victory;
Does not speak but is good at responding;
Does not call but things come of their own accord;
Is not anxious but is good at laying plans.
Heaven's net is vast;
Its mesh is loose but misses nothing.

Chapter Seventy-four

If the people are not afraid of death, why threaten them with
        death?
    "But what if I could keep the people always afraid of
        death,
    And seize and put to death those who dare to act in
        strange or perverse ways?
    Who then would dare to act in such a manner?"[151]
There is always the killing done by the Chief Executioner.[152]
The Chief Executioner is the greatest carver among
        carpenters.
Those who would do the work of the greatest carver among
        carpenters,
    rarely avoid wounding their own hands.

Chapter Seventy-five

The people are hungry because those above eat up too much
in taxes;
This is why the people are hungry.
The people are difficult to govern because those above
engage in action;
This is why the people are difficult to govern.
People look upon death lightly because those above are
obsessed with their own lives;[153]
This is why the people look upon death lightly.
Those who do not strive to live are more worthy than those
who cherish life.

Chapter Seventy-six

When alive human beings are supple and weak;
When dead they are stiff and strong.
When alive the myriad creatures, plants, and trees are supple
          and weak;
When dead they are withered and dry.
And so the stiff and the strong are the disciples of death;[154]
The supple and weak are the disciples of life.
This is why,
     A weapon that is too strong will not prove victorious;
     A tree that is too strong will break.
The strong and the mighty reside down below;
The soft and the supple reside on top.[155]

Chapter Seventy-seven

The Way of Heaven, is it not like the stretching of a bow?
What is high it presses down;
What is low it lifts up.
It takes from what has excess;
It augments what is deficient.
The Way of Heaven takes from what has excess and
        augments what is deficient.
The Way of human beings is not like this.
It takes from the deficient and offers it up to those with
        excess.
Who is able to offer what they have in excess to the world?
Only one who has the Way!
This is why sages act with no expectation of reward.[156]
When their work is done, they do not linger.[157]
They do not desire to make a display of their worthiness.

Chapter Seventy-eight

In all the world, nothing is more supple or weak than water;
Yet nothing can surpass it for attacking what is stiff and
        strong.
And so nothing can take its place.
That the weak overcomes the strong and the supple
        overcomes the hard,
These are things everyone in the world knows but none can
        practice.
This is why sages say,
    Those who can take on the disgrace of the state
    Are called lords of the altar to the soil and grain.[158]
    Those who can take on the misfortune of the state,
    Are called kings of all the world.[159]
Straightforward words seem paradoxical.

Chapter Seventy-nine

In cases of great resentment, even when resolution is reached,
　　　　some resentment remains.
How can this be considered good?
This is why sages maintain the left hand portion of the
　　　　tally,[160]
But do not hold people accountable.
Those with Virtue oversee the tally;
Those without Virtue oversee collection.[161]
The Way of Heaven plays no favorites;
It is always on the side of the good.

Chapter Eighty

Reduce the size of the state;
Lessen the population.
Make sure that even though there are labor saving tools, they
are never used.
Make sure that the people look upon death as a weighty
matter and never move to distant places.
Even though they have ships and carts, they will have no use
for them.
Even though they have armor and weapons, they will have no
reason to deploy them.
Make sure that the people return to the use of the knotted
cord.[162]
Make their food savory,
Their clothes fine,
Their houses comfortable,
Their lives happy.
Then even though neighboring states are within sight of
each other,
Even though they can hear the sounds of each other's dogs
and chickens,
Their people will grow old and die without ever having
visited one another.

Chapter Eighty-one

Words worthy of trust are not beautiful;
Words that are beautiful are not worthy of trust.[163]
The good do not engage in disputation;
Those who engage in disputation are not good.[164]
Those who know are not full of knowledge;
Those full of knowledge do not know.
Sages do not accumulate.
The more they do for others, the more they have;
The more they give to others, the more they possess.
The Way of Heaven is to benefit and not harm.
The Way of the sage is to act but not contend.

NOTES TO TRANSLATION

1. Unlike the case of the following line, which has a similar basic structure, there is no way to reproduce in English the alternating nominal and verbal uses of the word *dao* 道, "Way." More literally, the first line reads, *dao* 道, [a] "Way," "path," or " teaching," *kedao* 可道, [which] "can be talked about" or "followed," *fei changdao* 非常道, "is not a constant Way." Cf. the grammar and sense of the poem, "The Thorny Bush Upon the Wall," in the *Book of Odes* (*Mao # 46*). For a translation, see Legge 1970, 74–75. For other passages that discuss the Way and names, see, for example, chapters 32 and 34.

2. On the idea of being "nameless," see chapters 32, 37, and 41.

3. Cf. the reference to *xuantong* 玄同, "Enigmatic Unity," in chapter 56.

4. The point is the common theme that self-conscious effort to be excellent in any way fatally undermines itself. Cf. chapters 38 and 81.

5. Cf. chapter 40.

6. For *wuwei* 無為, "nonaction," see Slingerland (forthcoming).

7. Cf. a similar line in chapter 43.

8. Cf. chapter 34.

9. This line also occurs in chapters 10 and 51.

10. This line also appears in chapters, 10, 51, and 77.

11. Recognizing that the credit for their success lies with the Way and not with themselves is a characteristic attitude of Daoist sages. For similar ideas, see chapters 9, 17, 34, and 77. This and the previous line occur together in chapter 77.

12. For other passages discussing "precious goods," see chapters 12 and 64.

13. In *Analects* 12.18, Kongzi responds to Ji Kangzi, the leader of a powerful clan who was distressed over the number of thieves in his state, by saying, "If only you sir did not desire [such things], others would not steal even if you re-

warded them." For a complete translation of the passage see Waley 1938, 167.

14. The character *xin* 心, "heart" or "mind," can refer to the physical organ in the chest, but it most often refers to the psychological faculties of thinking, perceiving, feeling, desiring, or intending.

15. The following four lines appear in chapter 56 preceded by two lines from chapter 52.

16. This is the only occurrence in the text of the character *di* 帝, "Supreme Spirit," a name for the high god or supreme ancestral spirit of ancient China. For other passages concerning *xiang* 象, "image," see chapters 14, 21, 35, and 41.

17. "Straw dogs" were used as ceremonial offerings. Before and during the ceremony, they were protected and cherished, but as soon as the ceremony ended, they were discarded and defiled. Others interpret the characters in this expression as "straw and dogs." The point is the same.

18. Cf. the opening lines of chapter 23.

19. These seven lines make the point that our conception of the good is relative to different kinds of things, situations, relationships, and activities. Compare this to Aristotle's view that there is no Platonic "Good" that all good things share or partake of; rather, each is good *of its kind* (see *Nicomachean Ethics*, 1094a–1100a). The *Daodejing* also expresses the belief that the good of each creature and thing in the world is realized only when all play their proper roles in the greater harmony that is the *dao*.

20. The reference is to a tilting vessel that would fall over and pour out its contents if filled to the top. The Warring States Period Confucian philosopher Xunzi describes this vessel in chapter 28 of the work that bears his name. For a translation, see Knoblock 1994, 244.

21. For similar lines, see chapters 2, 17, 34, and 77.

22. For other examples of "the One," see chapters 22, 39, and 42.

23. The term *qi* 氣 refers to mist or vapor in general and human breath in particular. It also has come to have the

more technical sense of a kind of vital energy, found in both the atmosphere and within the human body and existing in various densities and levels of clarity or turbidity, that is responsible for, among other things, the intensity of one's emotions, one's mood, energy level and general health. Cf. notes 85 and 110.

24. Because of their graphic similarity, *xuanlan* 玄覽, "enigmatic vision," has been read as *xuanjian* 玄鑒 "enigmatic mirror," by a number of translators. This would be the only instance of the use of the metaphor of the "mind as a mirror" in the text and since it can be read without emendation, I have not altered the original. However, the "mind as a mirror" metaphor is developed in interesting ways in the *Zhuangzi*. For a discussion of this issue in the latter text, see Carr and Ivanhoe 2000, 38 and 56.

25. This line also appears in chapters 2 and 51.

26. This line also appears in chapters 2, 51, and 77.

27. Chapter 51 concludes with the same four lines. For another passage concerning *xuande* 玄德, "Enigmatic Virtue," see chapter 65.

28. Literally, only by relying on "nothing" (i.e., the empty space of the hub) can the wheel turn and the carriage roll.

29. These sets of five refer to conventional standards of evaluation with regard to the different sensory faculties. The passage is not a rejection of the pleasures of the senses, nor does it express skepticism regarding the senses per se. Rather, like the view one finds in chapter 2 of the *Zhuangzi*, it expresses a profound distrust of conventional categories and values and advocates moderation of sensual pleasures. For a translation of the *Zhuangzi*, see Graham 2001, 48–61. Cf. *Zhuangzi*, chapter 10; Graham 2001, 208–9.

30. This line also appears in chapters 38 and 72.

31. Cf. the thought expressed in these lines to what one finds in chapter 35.

32. Returning to an ideal past state is a common theme in the text. For other examples, see chapters 16, 25, 28, 52.

The time "before there were things" refers to the age of natural spontaneity, when people simply responded to whatever situation was before them without relying on fixed and definite schemes of discrimination or evaluation.

33. For other passages that concern *xiang* 象, "image," see chapters 4, 21, 35, and 41.

34. *Pu* 朴, "unhewn wood," is a symbol for anything in its unadulterated natural state. In other contexts I will translate it as "simplicity," but here and in certain later passages the metaphor is an important part of the passage's sense. For other examples, see chapters 19, 28, 32, 37, and 57.

35. Here and in certain other passages, we get a fleeting glimpse of the first-person narrator, the author of at least this line of the text. For other examples, see chapters 20, 25, 37, 69, and 70.

36. This line also appears in chapter 52.

37. This line appears again in chapter 23. I interpret it as an expression of the *Daodejing's* characteristic view on *de*, "Virtue." For a discussion of the idea of "Virtue" in the *Daodejing* and how it differs from related Confucian conceptions of "Virtue" or "moral charisma," see my "The Concept of *de* ('Virtue') in the *Laozi*," in Csikszentmihalyi and Ivanhoe 1998, 239–57. For other passages concerning the concept of trust, see chapters 49 and 63.

38. Sages are reluctant and slow to speak, but their words are worthy of complete trust.

39. Cf. chapters 2, 9, 34, and 77.

40. Literally, "We are this way *ziran* 自然." For other examples, see chapters 23, 25, 51, and 64.

41. The idea that more can lead to less and its implication that less can yield more is a theme that appears in several places in the text. For examples, see chapters 19 and 38. This passage expresses the general theme that the self-conscious appreciation of virtue is a mark of the decline of the *dao*. Here we also see an expression of the idea that

the world has fallen out of an earlier, ideal state of being.
42. Literally, "unhewn wood." See n. 34.
43. I take this to be saying not that one should fear what most people find fearful by as it were commanding oneself to be afraid of it, but rather that one should find the fact that everyone fears a certain thing as a legitimate source of apprehension.
44. In this passage, the author enters into an autobiographical mode. See also chapters 16, 25, 37, 69, and 70.
45. For other passages concerning *xiang*, "image," see 4, 14, 35, and 41.
46. For other examples of "the One," see chapters 10, 39, and 42.
47. See chapter 24 for a set of lines similar to the preceding four.
48. The same line appears in chapter 66.
49. While the *Daodejing* does not cite ancient sages or texts by name, here and elsewhere it clearly does quote ancient sources. For other examples, see chapters 42, 62, and 69.
50. The same line appears in chapter 17. See n. 37.
51. See chapter 22 for a set of lines similar to the preceding four.
52. A similar line appears in chapter 31.
53. There is a play here on the difference between one's *ming* 名, "proper name," and one's *zi* 字, "style." In traditional Chinese society one does not use the former, personal name in public. And so the author can be understood as saying he is not intimately familiar with the *dao* and so knows only its style, or perhaps that it would be unseemly to speak its true and proper name to those unfamiliar with it. Here we find another example of the first-person narrator. For other examples, see chapters, 16, 20, 37, 69, and 70.
54. Cf. The description of the Way found in chapter 6 of the *Zhuangzi*: "As for the Way, it is something with identity, something to trust in, but does nothing, has no shape. It can be handed down but not taken as one's own, can be grasped but not seen. Itself the trunk, itself the root,

since before there was a heaven and an earth inherently from of old it is what it was. It hallows ghosts and hallows God, engenders heaven engenders earth; it is farther than the upmost pole but is not reckoned high, it is under the six-way-oriented but is not reckoned deep, it is born before heaven and earth but is not reckoned long-lasting, it is elder to the most ancient but is not reckoned old," Graham 2001, 86.

55. "Natural" is *ziran*.

56. Cf. chapter 45.

57. Cf. chapter 62.

58. The expression *ximing* 襲明, "inheriting enlightenment," is open to numerous interpretations. I take it as describing the good that bad people inherit from those who already are enlightened.

59. Or "simplicity." See n. 34.

60. *Qi* 器, "vessel," "implement," or "tool," is a common metaphor for a government official. Playing on this image, it carries the slightly negative connotation of someone with limited "capacity." In *Analects* 2.12, Kongzi insists, "A gentleman never serves as a tool." Cf. Waley 1938, 90. See also *Analects* 5.3; Waley 1938, 107.

61. For *qu tianxia* 取天下, "gaining the world," see chapters 48 and 57.

62. These two lines also appear in chapter 64.

63. The final three lines also appear at the end of chapter 55.

64. The left side being associated with happy and auspicious events and the right side with sad and inauspicious events.

65. On the idea of being "nameless," see chapters 1, 37, and 41.

66. Or "simplicity." See n. 34.

67. Cf. the similar line in chapter 44.

68. For the value of *zu* 足, "contentment," see chapters 44 and 46.

69. Cf. the teaching quoted in chapter 42.

70. Cf. chapter 2.

71. Cf. chapters 2, 9, 17, and 77.

72.   Literally, one could *ming* 名, "name," or "call" it small.

73.   For other passages that concern *xiang* 象, "image," see chapters 4, 14, 21, and 41.

74.   The proper sense of *liqi* 利器, "sharp implements," is a matter of considerable controversy. Whether it refers to the weapons of the state, its ministers, labor-saving tools, the Daoist sage, or something else is hard to say, so I have left it ambiguous. Cf. the use in chapter 57. This line is quoted and explained in chapter 10 of the *Zhuangzi*. In his translation, Angus Graham does not include the quote of the line but does translate the explanation of it, "The sage is the sharpest tool of the empire, he is not a means of bringing light to the empire." See Graham 2001, 208.

75.   Cf. the similar line in chapter 48.

76.   For the notion of creatures "transforming themselves," see chapter 57.

77.   Or "nameless simplicity." See n. 34. On the idea of being "nameless," see chapters 1, 32, and 41. This line employs the first-person narrator perspective. For other examples, see chapters 16, 20, 25, 69, and 70.

78.   The word rendered here as "ritually correct" is *li* 禮, which in other contexts is translated as "having propriety."

79.   This line also appears in chapters 12 and 72.

80.   For other examples of "the One," see chapters 10, 22, and 42.

81.   The same expressions occur in chapter 42.

82.   For other passages that concern *xiang* 象, "image," see chapters 4, 14, 21, 35, and 41.

83.   On the idea of being "nameless," see chapters 1, 32, and 37.

84.   The precise referents of these terms are hard to determine. I take the Way to be the most inclusive term designating the hidden, underlying structure of things. The "One" would then be its *xiang* 象, "image," the closest thing we can have to a picture or representation of the Way. (For other examples, see chapters 10, 22, and 39.)

The "two" would then be the fundamental *qi* 氣, "vital energies," *yin* 陰 and *yang* 陽 (Cf. notes 24 and 110). These, together with our image of the Way as a unified whole, give rise to everything in the world. A similar scheme is described in the appendices to the *Book of Changes*. See Wilhelm 1952, 273–81. This process, whatever its particulars, was understood as a natural progression. There was no creator and the "nothing" out of which things arose is a primal state of undifferentiated vital energy, the state of no things but not absolute Nothingness. In ancient Greece, Anaximander proposed a similar scheme in which the fundamental forces of heat and cold arise out of an indefinite and boundless original state. Thanks to Eirik L. Harris for suggesting this comparison.

85. See chapter 39.

86. Cf. the similar line in chapter 2.

87. For the value of "contentment," see chapters 33 and 46.

88. Cf. the similar line in chapter 32.

89. Very close to the city, thus showing a heightened state of mobilization.

90. For the value of "contentment," see chapters 33 and 44.

91. I take the point here and in several other passages concerning "contentment" to be something close to what contemporary philosophers call "satisficing." The idea is that the effort expended in always seeking to maximize one's satisfaction often offers dramatically diminishing returns and is not in fact in the agent's overall best interests. The *Daodejing* claims that a satisficing strategy is not only better for individual agents but for the world at large because a focus on being content will lead people away from the competitive and frenetic pursuits that characterize much of human life. For the notion of "satisficing," see Herbert A. Simon, *Models of Bounded Rationality* (Cambridge, Mass: MIT Press, 1982), and Michael A. Slote, *Beyond Optimizing: A Study of Rational Choice* (Cambridge, Mass: Harvard University Press, 1989).

92. That is until one reaches the state of *wuwei* 無爲, "nonaction."

93. Cf. the similar lines in chapter 37.

94. For *wushi* 無事, "no activity," see chapters 57 and 63. For *qu tianxia*, "gaining the world," see chapters 29 and 57.

95. I read this line, and the line three lines below it, as playing on the etymological and semantic relationship between *de* 德, "Virtue," and *de* 得, "to get." Since those with Virtue naturally are good to and trust others, they accrue ("get") Virtue; this enables them to gain ("get") the support of others and realize ("get") their greater ends. Cf. chapters 17, 23, and 38. For a revealing discussion of the early Chinese concept of *de*, see David S. Nivison's "*Virtue* in Bone and Bronze" and "The Paradox of Virtue," both in Nivison 1996, 17–43.

96. Cf. chapter 76.

97. This passage has been interpreted in a wide variety of ways. I take its general theme to be the preservation of one's natural span of life, here connected to the idea that wanting something too badly often leads to its opposite. Some are fated to live long and others to die young. However, about one in three brings misfortune on himself. The missing person in ten is of course the sage. By not doing, sages avoid creating a place for death to enter in.

98. Cf. chapter 75.

99. This line also appears in chapters 2 and 10.

100. This line also appears in chapters 2, 10, and 77.

101. Chapter 10 concludes with these same four lines. For *xuande*, "Enigmatic Virtue," see chapter 65.

102. This line also appears in chapter 16.

103. This and the preceding line also appear in chapter 56.

104. Cf. *Analects* 6.12, where Kongzi commends a man for "never taking a shortcut." For a full translation of the passage, see Waley 1938, 118.

105. "It" refers to the Way. Note that in this and the following lines the word translated as "Virtue" also clearly has the sense of a kind of "power."

106. The progression from cultivating the Way in oneself to

cultivating it throughout the empire is reminiscent of the progression one sees in chapter 4 of the *Daxue* 大學, "Great Learning," a work primarily associated with Confucianism. There we are told that those who wish to "make bright their shining Virtue throughout the world" must first "order their states." Those who wish to order their states must first "regulate their families," those who wish to regulate their families must first "cultivate themselves," and so on. Wing-tsit Chan points out that Mengzi ("Mencius") identifies this basic idea as a "common saying" in *Mengzi* 4A5. See Chan 1963, 196. For a translation of the *Mengzi*, see Lau 1970, 120.

107. The early Confucian Mengzi also uses the newborn as an image for his ideal state of mind. In *Mengzi* 4B12, he claims, "The great man is he who never loses the heart of a child." Cf. Lau 1970, 130.

108. Cf. the closing lines of chapter 5 of the *Zhuangzi*, where Zhuangzi says, "Follow the natural and do not *yisheng* 益生, 'help life along.'" Cf. Graham 2001, 82.

109. Early Daoists tended to advocate allowing one's vital energies to find their natural course. For example, see the "fasting of the heart and mind" passage in chapter 4 of the *Zhuangzi* (see Graham 2001, 66–69). They were opposed to those such as the early Confucian Mengzi, who argued that the mind should guide the vital energies. See Mengzi's discussion of nourishing the "flood-like *qi*" in *Mengzi* 2A2. See Lau 1970, 77–78.

110. The final three lines also appear at the end of chapter 30.

111. I take the implied subject to be the *dao*.

112. This and the preceding line also appear together in chapter 52.

113. This and the preceding three lines also appear together in chapter 4.

114. Cf. chapter 1, "Their unity is known as an enigma."

115. This line also appears in chapter 62.

116. For *wushi*, "no activity," see chapters 48 and 63. For *qu tianxia* 取天下, "gaining the world," see chapters 29 and 48.

117.   For the expression "sharp implements," see chapter 36.

118.   Cf. chapter 37.

119.   Literally "unhewn wood." See n. 34.

120.   The idea is that too much attention and meddling will make either fall apart.

121.   Laozi seems here to be arguing against the idea, seen in thinkers like Mozi et al., that the ideal state requires the active participation of ghosts and other spirits in meting out rewards or punishments. Laozi does not deny the existence of such beings but like Kongzi sees a direct appeal to them as inappropriate. Cf. Kongzi's advice concerning ghosts and spirits in *Analects* 6.22: "Respect ghosts and spirits but keep them at a distance." For a full translation of the passage, see Waley 1938, 120.

122.   They do not disturb the people through too much attention and meddling.

123.   Literally *xialiu* 下流, "low flow." Cf. the use of the same term in *Analects* 19.20: "the gentleman dislikes living in low places (*xialiu*) where all the foul things under Heaven collect." The Daoist of course inverts Confucian values, esteeming what the world regards as lowly. For a full translation of the passage, see Waley 1938, 228.

124.   In the sense that the ideal great state places itself below and attracts the whole world. Also, like a valley or the delta of a river, the great state is like a woman in being fertile and having the ability to feed the whole world. Cf. chapter 66.

125.   "Inner sanctum" is the translation of *ao* 奧, the southwest corner of one's house where the household gods are lodged and worshipped.

126.   Cf. chapter 81.

127.   Cf. chapter 27.

128.   Cf. Mozi's discussion of how the Son of Heaven and three high ministers are to be appointed, in chapter 2 of the *Mozi*. For a translation, see Watson 1963, 34–35.

129.   This line also appears in chapter 56.

130.   For *wushi* 無事, "no activities," see chapters 48 and 57.

131.   The idea in each case is that one should do what one

does in unpremeditated and spontaneous response to the situation at hand. One should do away with set schemes, categories, standards, and plans and follow one's natural inclinations and tendencies. And so, for example, one should taste and savor what one finds pleasing, not what others might enjoy or what accords with some socially sanctioned view about good taste. Cf. chapter 12. This idea is explored at some length in chapter 10 of the *Zhuangzi*. See Graham 2001, 208–9.

132. Here we see a clear contrast with the view of early Confucians. In *Analects* 14.34, Kongzi is asked specifically about the practice of repaying resentment with Virtue. He rejects it and instead advocates that one "Repay resentment with uprightness." For a full translation of the passage, see Waley 1938, 189. Cf. chapter 49.

133. These two lines also appear in chapter 29.

134. Cf. *Mengzi* 7 B35, "For cultivating the heart and mind nothing is better than to make few one's desires." For a full translation of the passage, see Lau 1970, 210–12.

135. Daoist sages take Nature as their model. In philosophical discussions of the time, there was a debate about whether the proper content of learning is part of or opposed to what is naturally so. This debate in turn was a reflection of a larger debate about the character of human nature. Mengzi endorses only particular natural tendencies—those that incline us toward morality—and on this basis claims that human nature is good. Xunzi argues that our untutored nature inclines us toward bad states of affairs. On this basis he concludes that our nature is bad and must be reformed through protracted study and practice. We can see Laozi, Mengzi, and Xunzi as representing a spectrum of views about the proper content of learning that reflects their different views about the goodness of our prereflective nature, running from greatest to least confidence in our raw natural state.

136. The idea that the best of actions flow forth without reflection or knowledge was not uncommon in early China. In his note on this line, Wing-tsit Chan cites a

passage from the *Book of Odes* in which the Supreme Spirit or Lord on High commends King Wen for his behavior: "Without reflection or knowledge, you comply with my principles" (*Mao* #241). See Chan 1963, 216. For a translation of the ode, see Legge 1970, 454. Cf. *Analects* 15.4. For a translation of the *Analects* passage, see Waley 1938, 193.

137. For *xuande* 玄德, "Enigmatic Virtue," see chapters 10 and 51.

138. This is the only occurrence of the expression *dashun* 大順, "Great Compliance," in the text. However, as Arthur Waley points out in his note to this chapter, it does occur in *Zhuangzi*, chapter 12. See Waley 1963, 223. For the reference in the *Zhuangzi*, see Graham 2001, 156 (who translates these characters as "ultimate course"). Note too that the same word *shun* appears in *Mao* #241, quoted in n. 136 above.

139. Cf. chapter 61.

140. The same line appears in chapter 22.

141. The idea that true virtue lies in a harmony within a tension, that it requires a balance between extremes, is seen in many traditions. Early Confucians too held a version of this view. For example, *Analects* 8.2 tells us, "Respect without ritual propriety becomes laborious bustle. Care without ritual propriety becomes timidity. Courage without ritual propriety becomes disorderliness. Straightforwardness without ritual propriety becomes rudeness." Cf. Waley 1938, 132.

142. That is, they are not overly aggressive and pugnacious.

143. They avoid initiating the action, the first move being the prerogative of the host.

144. Cf. the last two lines with line 7 of chapter 38.

145. See chapter 67 for a possible reference. Note that here we see the perspective of the first-person narrator. For other examples, see chapters 16, 20, 25, 37, and 70.

146. Several lines in this chapter employ the perspective of the first-person narrator. For other examples, see chapters 16, 20, 25, 37, 69, and 70.

147. Cf. this complaint with Kongzi's remark in *Analects* 14.37: "No one understands me—is this not so?" For a full translation of the passage, see Waley 1938, 189.

148. They appear common and unworthy on the outside but possess a secret treasure within. In *Analects* 17.1, a man named Yang Huo criticizes Kongzi's reluctance to take office by asking him, "Can one who cherishes his treasure within and allows his state to go astray be considered benevolent?" Cf. *Analects* 9.12 and 15.6. For full translations of these passages, see Waley 1938, 141, 194, and 209.

149. Cf. *Analects* 2.17: "If you know something realize that you know it. If you do not know something realize that you do not. This is what knowing is." For a full translation of the passage, see Waley 1938, 91.

150. This line also appears in chapters 12 and 38.

151. These two lines introduce a question and mark a dialogue within the text. Cf. *Analects* 12.19, in which Ji Kangzi asks Kongzi, "What about putting to death those who are without the Way in order to advance those who have it?" For a full translation of the passage, see Waley 1938, 168.

152. The death that Heaven brings to each person.

153. Cf. chapter 50.

154. Cf. chapter 50.

155. The Han Dynasty commentator Wang Bi illustrates the point of these last two lines with the examples of the roots of a tree and its twigs.

156. This line also appears in chapters 2, 10, and 51.

157. Cf. chapters 2, 9, 17, and 34. This and the previous line also appear together in chapter 2.

158. These were the main altars of the state and a common metaphor for its independence and well-being.

159. The idea that the most worthy rulers are willing to offer themselves to Heaven as surrogates on behalf of the people and in the name of the state is a motif seen in writings of this period and earlier. See Nivison 1996, 20–24. See also King Tang's pronouncement to the spirits in the

Analects 20.1. For a translation of this passage, see Waley 1938, 231–32.

160. The left-hand portion of a contract of obligation, the part that was held by the creditor.

161. The central idea of this chapter, which is also seen throughout the text, is that one cannot force others to be good. If one resorts to force, one's actions will eventually rebound in kind upon oneself. The only way to affect others and turn them to the good is through the power of one's *de*, "Virtue."

162. That is, let them abandon writing. The use of the knotted cord to keep track of records is mentioned in the Great Appendix to the *Book of Changes* and chapter 10 of the *Zhuangzi*, as well as elsewhere in the early literature. For the Great Appendix, see Wilhelm 1952, 360. For the reference in the *Zhuangzi*, see Graham 2001, 209.

163. In *Analects* 14.6, Kongzi says, "Those who have *de*, 'Virtue,' will always have something to say. Those who have something to say will not always have Virtue." Cf. chapter 62. For a full translation of the *Analects* passage, see Waley 1938, 180.

164. Confucians too had a general mistrust of glib talkers and disputation. This reflects their similar though distinct beliefs about the power of a good person's *de*, "Virtue," to sway others. For examples, see *Analects* 1.3 and Mengzi's explanation of why he must engage in disputation, though not being fond of it, found in *Mengzi* 3B9. For a translation of the *Analects* passage, see Waley 1938, 84; for the passage from the *Mengzi*, see Lau 1970, 113–15.

Language Appendix

Below is the original Chinese text of the first chapter of the *Daodejing*, followed by eight English translations.[1] All of these are by eminent translators and have enjoyed considerable popularity among Western audiences. In the exercise that follows, I show how each translator interpreted the text by explaining the grammatical, semantic, or philosophical assumptions underlying his English rendering of the text.

I offer this appendix as a way for readers to pull back at least part of the veil that obscures the act of translation and to give them at least some sense of what it is like to move from classical Chinese to modern English. I hope too that it will show that there are many plausible ways to construe the language of the *Daodejing*. Once the grammatical and semantic issues have all been explored, there is still much interpretative work to be done. Issues concerning historical context, consistency, or philosophical vision will then play important roles in how one renders a given line.

I. THE ORIGINAL TEXT[2]

道可道，非常道。
名可名，非常名。
無名天地之始；
有名萬物之母。
故常無欲，以觀其妙；
常有欲，以觀其徼。
此兩者，同出而異名，
同謂之玄。
玄之又玄，
眾妙之門。

II. Eight English Translations

1. Legge, James. *The Texts of Taoism.*

The Dao that can be trodden is not the enduring and
   unchanging Dao.
The name that can be named is not the enduring and
   unchanging name.
[Conceived of as] having no name, it is the Originator of
   heaven and earth;
[Conceived of as] having a name, it is the Mother of all
   things.
  Always without desire we must be found
  If its deep mystery we would sound;
  But if desire always within us be,
  Its outer fringe is all that we shall see.
Under these two aspects it is really the same; but as
   development takes place it receives different names.
   Together we call them the Mystery. Where the
   Mystery is the deepest is the gate of all that is subtle
   and wonderful.

2. Lin, Yutang. *The Wisdom of China and India.*

The Dao that can be told of is not the Absolute Dao;
The Names that can be given are not Absolute Names.
The Nameless is the origin of Heaven and Earth;
The Named is the Mother of All Things.
Therefore:
  Oftentimes, one strips oneself of passion
  In order to see the Secret of Life;
  Oftentimes, one regards life with passion

In order to see its manifest results.
These two [the Secret and its manifestations]
Are [in their nature] the same;
They are given different names
When they become manifest.
They may both be called the Cosmic Mystery:
Reaching from the Mystery into the Deeper Mystery
Is the Gate to the Secret of All Life.

3. Waley, Arthur. *The Way and Its Power.*

The Way that can be told of is not an Unvarying Way;
The names that can be named are not unvarying names.
It was from the Nameless that Heaven and Earth sprang;
The named is but the mother that rears the ten thousand
        creatures, each after its kind.
Truly, "Only he that rids himself forever of desire can see the
        Secret Essences";
He that has never rid himself of desire can see only the
        Outcomes.
These two things issue from the same mould, but
        nevertheless are different in name.
This "same mould" we can but call the Mystery,
Or rather the "Darker than any Mystery,"
The Doorway whence issued all Secret Essences.

4. Duyvendak, J.J.L. *Tao Te Ching.*

The Way that may truly be regarded as the Way is other than
        a permanent Way.
The terms that may truly be regarded as terms are other than
        permanent terms.

The term Non-being indicates the beginning of heaven and
        earth;
The term Being indicates the mother of the ten thousand
        things.
For, indeed, it is through the constant alternation between
        Non-being and Being that the wonder of the one
        and limitation of the other will be seen.
These two, having a common origin, are named with
        different terms.
What they have in common is called the Mystery,
The Mystery of Mysteries, the Gate of all Wonders.

5. Chan, Wing-tsit. *The Way of Lao Tzu.*

The Dao that can be told of is not the eternal Dao;
The name that can be named is not the eternal name.
The Nameless is the origin of Heaven and Earth;
The Named is the mother of all things.
Therefore, let there always be non-being, so we may see their
        subtlety,
And let there always be being, so we may see their outcome.
The two are the same,
But after they are produced they have different names.
They both may be called deep and profound.
Deeper and more profound,
The door of all subtleties!

6. Lau, D.C. *Lao Tzu: Tao Te Ching.*

The way that can be spoken of
Is not the constant way;
The name that can be named

Is not the constant name.
The nameless was the beginning of heaven and earth;
The named was the mother of the myriad creatures.
Hence always rid yourself of desires in order to observe its
    secrets;
But always allow yourself to have desires in order to observe
    its manifestations.
These two are the same
But diverge in name as they issue forth.
Being the same they are called mysteries,
Mystery upon mystery—
The gateway of the manifold secrets.

7. Welch, Holmes. *Taoism: The Parting of the Way.*

The Dao that can be Dao'd is not the Absolute Dao;
The name that can be named is not the absolute name.
It was from the nameless that Heaven and Earth sprang;
The named is but the mother of the Ten Thousand
    Creatures.*
Truly, "Only he that rids himself forever of desire can see the
    Secret Essences,"
He that has never rid himself of desire can see only the
    Outcomes.
These two things issued from the same mould, but
    nevertheless are different in name.
This "same mould" we can but call the Mystery,
Or rather the "Darker than any Mystery,"
The Doorway whence issued all Secret Essences.

-----

*Welch follows Waley in his translation of the remaining
    six lines.

8. Feng, Gai-fu, and Jane English. *Lao Tzu: Tao Te Ching.*

The Dao that can be told is not the eternal Dao.
The name that can be named is not the eternal name.
The nameless is the beginning of heaven and earth.
The named is the mother of the ten thousand things.
Ever desireless, one can see the mystery.
Ever desiring, one can see the manifestations.
These two spring from the same source but differ in name;
    this appears as darkness.
Darkness within darkness.
The gate to all mystery.

III. LINE-BY-LINE ROMANIZATION, TRANSLATION, AND EXPLANATION OF EACH INTERPRETATION

Line 1: (Lines 1 and 2 will be discussed together.)

道	可	道	非	常	道
dao	*ke*	*dao*	*fei*	*chang*	*dao*
way	can	way	not	constant	way

Line 2:

名	可	名	非	常	名
ming	*ke*	*ming*	*fei*	*chang*	*ming*
name	can	name	not	constant	name

Most of the important differences among translators in regard to Line 1 concern the character *dao* 道. While the exact etymology of this character remains obscure, one of the basic meanings of its early forms was a physical path. There is considerable overlap with the semantic range of this character and the English word "way." Like its English correlate, *dao* came to refer more generally to a way of doing something, an oral or written account of such a way, and, when used as a verb, to the provision of such an account. In certain contexts it can also mean to follow some path or teaching or simply to regard or take such a path or teaching as one's own. Depending on the context, the *dao* in question can be *a* way of doing something, or it can refer to *the* right way. Daoists use the term to refer to what is responsible for the overall, underlying pattern of the universe.

In this line, the character *dao* is used first as a nominal, meaning the *Way*. Next it is used as a verb; this is handled in different ways by the various translators. Welch approaches the problem by *verbalizing* the transliteration of the character as "dao'd." Lin, Waley, Chan, Lau, and Feng render it "to speak or tell of." Duyvendak takes it to mean "to regard as the Dao" while Legge opts for "trodden." The character appears for a third time in this line, again functioning as a nominal.

Our translators also show a range of opinions concerning how to render the character *chang* 常, which appears near the end of both Lines 1 and 2. It is translated as "constant," "eternal," "Unwavering," "permanent," "unchanging," and "Absolute." Notice how some translators resort to capitalization in this and other cases to add a specific nuance to their English translations. Another widely attested sense of the character *chang* is "common" or "everyday," though none of the translators in our sample understand it this way in the lines in question. The character appears again in Lines 5 and 6.

The grammar of Line 2 mirrors that of Line 1. Notice that this strong structural parallelism also occurs between Lines 3 and 4 and between Lines 5 and 6. Among the translations of Line 2, there is some difference of opinion in regard to the character *ming* 名. It is variously rendered as "name," "names," "terms." The character *ming* was at the center of a number of philosophical debates in early China regarding how exactly to fix the sense and reference of various "names" or "terms." There was the general problem of how *ming* related to *shi* 實, "stuff" or "reality." This is roughly the problem of reference. There was also a view, associated with the Confucian school, insisting that the sense of certain terms, especially those that were ethically normative, could be used to judge whether or not a given individual deserved to be regarded as a worthy representative of such types. For example, they insisted that part of the meaning of the term "king" was "someone who cares for his people." They used this point to argue that a cruel and tyrannical king was not *really* a king. Hence one did not owe such a person allegiance and in fact could drive him from power. The Daoist Zhuangzi questioned whether any term in fact had a reliable and stable relationship to reality. By implication, such a view questioned the entire edifice of traditional culture, which was based on making distinctions among various things and states of affairs—in particular among classes and types of people and various types of action.

Notice how the character *ming* reappears in Lines 3, 4, and 7 and how the translators handle these different occurrences of the same character.

Line 3: (Lines 3 and 4 will be discussed together.)

無	名	天	地	之	始
wu	*ming*	*tian*	*di*	*zhi*	*shi*
lack	name	heaven	earth	's*	beginning

Line 4:

有	名	萬	物	之	母
you	*ming*	*wan*	*wu*	*zhi*	*mu*
have	name	ten thousand	things	's*	mother

*This character serves as an attributive particle.

All but two of our translators agree that *wuming* 無名 in Line 3 is to be treated as a nominal lump or compound in apposition to the nominal phrase *tian di zhi shi* 天地之始. This structure is mirrored in Line 4, with *youming* 有名 standing in apposition to *wanwu zhi mu* 萬物之母. These two compounds are taken as the subjects, or topics, of these two sentences and translated into English as "the nameless" and "the named," respectively, by all of the translators in this group. (Note that Lin capitalizes "Names," "Nameless," and "Named," Waley capitalizes "Nameless," while Chan capitalizes "Nameless," and "Named.")

Duyvendak takes the character *wu* 無 in Line 3 and *you* 有 in Line 4 as if they were set off in quotation marks, with the character *ming* 名 serving as a verb meaning "to name" or "to indicate." He translates *wu* 無 as "non-being" and *you* 有 as "being," producing English sentences with the grammatical form of "X marks the spot."

Legge seems to want to emphasize that Lines 3 and 4 share a common referent (perhaps the *dao*?). Thus he interprets the characters *wu* 無 and *you* 有 as modifiers of the word *ming* 名, yielding "lacking name" and "having name," respectively. The bracketed phrase "Conceived of as" in each line, is interpolation.

Line 5: (Lines 5 and 6 will be discussed together.)

故	常	無	欲	以	觀	其	妙
gu	chang	wu	yu	yi	guan	qi	miao
And so	always	lack	desire	thereby	view	its	subtlety

Line 6:

常	有	欲	以	觀	其	徼
chang	you	yu	yi	guan	qi	jiao
always	have	desire	thereby	view	its	signs

The character *gu* 故 can be interpreted in at least two ways. It can be understood simply as "therefore" or "hence" as Lin, Chan, and Lau take it, or it can be understood as a shortened form of *gu yue* 故曰, "hence, it is said . . . ." Waley follows this latter line of interpretation, adding his own personal spin by treating Line 5 as a quote and Line 6 as a rejoinder or commentary on it.

There is another interpretive possibility that is worth noting. In Appendix Two (pages 172–73) to his translation of the *Daodejing*, D.C. Lau points out that, in texts of the late Warring States Period, the character *gu* 故 along with the characters *shi yi* 是以 often serve as a kind of textual glue. Authors or later editors used these characters to patch together and close the seams between originally unrelated passages, helping to give the appearance of continuity. The occurrence of the character *gu* 故 in this passage seems like a perfect candidate for such treatment. Note though that here and throughout his translation, Lau seldom makes use of this insight.

Legge is the only translator who preserves the original rhyme of these two lines. According to Bernard Kalgren, a scholar who has reconstructed the archaic pronunciation of many Chinese characters, these two characters were read as *miog* and *kiog*, respectively. They happen to retain their rhyme in modern Mandarin.

The character *chang* 常, which we saw earlier in Lines 1 and 2, is taken by Duyvendak as part of two compounds in Lines 5 and 6 and he merges these lines together in his translation. His juxtaposition of *chang wu* 常無 with *chang you* 常有 in the phrase "the constant alternation between Non-being and Being" probably was intended as an example of the notion of the interplay between the two primordial, vital energies *yin* and *yang*.

Like Duyvendak, Chan also takes *wu* 無 to mean "Non-being" and *you* 有 to mean "Being." On his interpretation the characters *yuyi* 欲以 are taken as an idiom, meaning "to tend or seek in this way [to do X]." Thus he understands the lines in something like the following way: "Hence let there always be Non-being and [in this way we may] see their subtlety."

Lau takes *wu* 無 in the causative sense, that is, "to cause not to have," and *yu* 欲 as "desires." Taken together, the meaning is, ". . . rid [yourself] of desires . . ."

Feng presents yet another alternative by taking *wu yu* 無欲 as a unit and translating it as "desirelessness." He employs a similar strategy with the characters *you yu* 有欲 in the following line.

Line 7:

此	兩	者	同	出	而	異	名
ci	*liang*	*zhe*	*tong*	*chu*	*er*	*yi*	*ming*
these	two	ones	same	come out	but	differ	name

The interpretation given to the character *tong* 同 and its relationship to the other characters in this line depends largely upon how one parses the line. There are at least two different possibilities. Legge, Lin, Chan, and Lau take the first option and split the line into two four-character sentences, *ci liang zhe tong* 此兩者同 and *chu er yi ming* 出而異名. On this reading the noun phrase *ci liang zhe* 此兩者, "These two," is the subject or topic of both sentences, referring either to "the Nameless and the Named" or to "Being and Non-being" (or possibly both). The character *tong* 同, "are the same," is the predicate of the first sentence. The phrase *chu er yi ming* 出而異名, "come out and then differ in name," is the predicate of the second sentence. This approach has the advantage of offering a pleasing symmetry.

Duyvendak, Waley, Feng, and Welch parse the line differently. They take it as a single sentence with *ci liang zhe* 此

兩者, "These two," as the subject or topic and *tong chu er yi ming* 同出而異名, "come out together but differ in name," as a complex predicate. This interpretation produces a symmetry of its own between *tong chu* 同出 and *yi ming* 異名.

Line 8:

同	謂	之	玄
tong	*wei*	*zhi*	*xuan*
same	call	this	darkness

The differences among our translators in regard to this line turn upon the way they handle the character *tong* 同. Lin and Chan interpret it as "both of these two," with "these two" referring to "the Nameless and the Named" or to "Being and Non-being" (or possibly both). Duyvendak, Waley, and Welch take *tong* as indicating what these two (whatever their referent) have in common, that is, their arising from "this same mould" or "common origin." Legge and Feng have yet another reading, understanding *tong* to mean "the two's being taken together."

Line 9:

玄	之	又	玄
xuan	*zhi*	*you*	*xuan*
darkness	's/to go	again/further	darkness

The character *zhi* 之 is interpreted as an attributive particle (as it functions in Lines 3 and 4 above) by all but one of our translators. Lin alone draws upon the character's verbal sense of "to go" or "to reach."

Line 10:

眾	妙	之	門
zhong	*miao*	*zhi*	*men*
many	darkness	's	gate

It seems fitting, or perhaps mysterious, that at the conclusion of chapter one, we find general agreement among our translators.

NOTES

1. In some of these translations, I have changed the romanization from the older Wade-Giles to the modern Pin-Yin system. So "Tao" becomes "Dao." However, I have left the citations in their original romanization in order to facilitate locating these texts.

2. In traditional texts, the characters are written vertically in columns starting from the right-hand side of the page. Many traditional texts have punctuation added that indicates major grammatical breaks in the text, but there are no special marks for distinguishing questions, imperatives, or declaratives. Manuscripts, such as those recently unearthed, have no punctuation at all. I have transcribed the text in horizontal lines starting from the top of the page and reading left to right. This is how most modern Chinese books are arranged.

Works Cited

Carr, Karen L., and Philip J. Ivanhoe. 2000. *The Sense of Antirationalism: The Religious Thought of Zhuangzi and Kierkegaard*. New York: Seven Bridges Press.

Chan, Alan K. 1991. *Two Visions of the Way: A study of the Wang Pi and the Ho-Shang Kung commentaries on the Lao-Tzu*. Albany: SUNY Press.

Chan, Wing-tsit, trans. 1963. *The Way of Lao Tzu (Tao te ching)*. Reprint. New York: Bobbs Merrill.

Craig, Edward, ed. 1998. *The Routledge Encyclopedia of Philosophy*, vol. 6. New York: Routledge.

Csikszentmihalyi, Mark, and Philip J. Ivanhoe, eds. 1999. *Religious and Philosophical Aspects of the Laozi*. Albany: SUNY Press.

Deutsch, Eliot, and Ronald Bontekoe, eds. 1997. *A Companion to World Philosophies*. Oxford: Blackwell.

Dyvendak, J.J.L. 1992. *Tao Te Ching*. Reprint. Rutland, Vt.: Charles E. Tuttle.

Feng, Gai-fu, and Jane English. 1970. *Lao Tzu: Tao Te Ching*. New York: Vintage Books.

Graham, Angus C., trans. 2001. *Chuang-Tzu: The Inner Chapters*. Reprint. Indianapolis: Hackett.

Hadot, Pierre. 1995. *Philosophy as a Way of Life*. Oxford: Blackwell.

Knoblock, John, trans. 1994. *Xunzi: A Translation and Study of the Complete Works, vol.* 3. Stanford: Stanford University Press.

Kohn, Livia, and Michael LaFargue, eds. 1998. *Lao-tzu and the Tao-te-ching*. Albany: SUNY Press.

Lau, D.C., trans. 1970. *Mencius*. Harmondsworth, England: Penguin Books.

Legge, James, trans. 1970. *The Chinese Classics, vol. 4, The She King*. Reprint. Hong Kong: Hong Kong University Press.

———. 1962. *The Texts of Taoism*. Reprint. New York: Dover Press.

Lin, Yutang. 1942. *The Wisdom of China and India*. New York: Random House.

Nivison, David S. 1996. *The Ways of Confucianism: Investigations in Chinese Philosophy*. La Salle, Ill.: Open Court.

Nussbaum, Martha C. 1994. *The Therapy of Desire: Theory and Practice in Hellenistic Ethics*. Princeton: Princeton University Press.

Slingerland, Edward G., III. Forthcoming. *Effortless Action: Wu-wei as Conceptual Metaphor and Spiritual Ideal in Early China*. New York: Oxford University Press.

Tucker, Mary Evelyn, and John Berthrong, eds. 1998. *Confucianism and Ecology: The Interrelation of Heaven, Earth, and Humans*. Cambridge, Mass.: Harvard University Press.

Wagner, Rudolf G. 2000. *The Craft of a Chinese Commentator: Wang Bi on the* Laozi. Albany: SUNY Press.

Waley, Arthur, trans. 1938. *The Analects of Confucius*. New York: Vintage Books.

———, trans. 1958. *The Way and Its Power*. New York: Grove Press.

Watson, Burton, trans. 1963. *Mo Tzu: Basic Writings*. New York: Columbia University Press.

Welch, Holmes. 1972. *Taoism: The Parting of the Way*. Reprint. Boston: Beacon Press.

Wilhelm, Richard. 1952. *The I Ching or Book of Changes*. New York: Pantheon Books.

Wright, Arthur F., ed. 1960. *The Confucian Persuasion*. Stanford: Stanford University Press.

Selected Bibliography

TRANSLATIONS

Chan, Alan K.L. 1991. *Two Visions of the Way*. Albany: SUNY Press. (A translation and study of the Heshanggong and Wang Bi commentaries on the *Laozi*.)

Chan, Wing-tsit. 1963. *The Way of Lao Tzu (Tao te ching)*. Chicago: University of Chicago Press. (A thoughtful and scholarly translation that makes revealing use of the commentarial tradition.)

Henricks, Robert G. 1989. *Lao-Tzu Te-Tao Ching*. New York: Ballantine. (A fine translation and introduction to the *Mawangdui* version of the text.)

Mair, Victor. 1990. *Tao Te Ching*. New York: Bantam Books. (An elegant and thoughtful translation and study of the *Mawangdui* version of the text.)

Lau, D.C. 1963. *Tao Te Ching*. Baltimore: Penguin Books. (A graceful and terse translation with informative introduction and appendices.)

Lynn, Richard John. 1999. *The Classic of the Way and Virtue: A New Translation of the Tao-Te Ching of Laozi as Interpreted by Wang Bi*. New York: Columbia University Press. (A masterful translation of the text and Wang Bi's commentary. Includes a thorough and insightful study of Wang Bi's life and thought.)

Waley, Arthur. 1963. *The Way and Its Power*. New York: Grove Press. (A thoughtful translation with a substantial and impressive introduction.)

SECONDARY WORKS

Creel, Herrlee G. 1970. *What Is Taoism? And Other Studies in Chinese Cultural History*. Chicago: University of Chicago Press. (Contains several seminal essays on the thought and history of the text.)

Csikszentmihalyi, Mark, and Philip J. Ivanhoe, eds. 1999. *Essays on Religious and Philosophical Aspects of the Laozi*. Albany:

SUNY Press. (An anthology of essays on the thought of the text.)

Kohn, Livia, and Michael LaFargue, eds. 1998. *Lao-tzu and the Tao-te-ching*. Albany: SUNY Press. (A broad range of essays on the text, its reception, and interpretation.)

Lau, D.C. 1958. "The Treatment of Opposites in Lao Tzu 老子," *Bulletin of the School of Oriental and African Studies* 21, pp. 344–60. (An intriguing exploration of one of the more paradoxical aspects of the text.)

GENERAL STUDIES OF CHINESE THOUGHT

Chan, Wing-tsit. 1963. *A Source Book in Chinese Philosophy*. Princeton: Princeton University Press.

Fung, Yu-lan. 1952–53. *A History of Chinese Philosophy*. Princeton: Princeton University Press.

Graham, Angus C. 1989. *Disputers of the Tao: Philosophical Argument in Ancient China*. La Salle, Ill.: Open Court.

Schwartz, Benjamin I. 1985. *The World of Thought in Ancient China*. Cambridge, Mass.: Belknap Press.

Index

spontaneity (*see also ziran*),
    xxii, 88, 96
state (the), 36, 57, 60, 62–64,
    68, 81, 83, 91, 95, 98
  in chaos, 18
  mother of the, 62
  altars of, 81, 98
  ordering of, 60, 94
  to rule, 68
stillness, 15–16, 37, 64
straw dogs, 5, 86
subtle, 14, 36
subtle enlightenment, 36
supple, 46
supreme commander, 31
Supreme Spirit, 4, 86, 97

taboos, 60
taxes, 78
teacher, 27
teaching, xxvii, 2, 45–46, 73
ten thousand creatures
    /things (the) (*see* myriad
    creatures)
three (the), 45
three ministers, 65, 95
three treasures (*see also* kind-
    ness; frugality; never
    putting oneself first), 70,
    72
tilting vessel, xvii, 9, 86
tool (*see also* vessel), 90
tools, labor-saving, 83, 91
Tucker, Mary Evelyn, xxxii
transforming, 37, 60, 91
troops, 60
trust, 17, 23, 52, 66, 84, 88, 93
trustworthy, 52

two (the), 45, 92

ulterior motives, 41
ultimate course, 97
undoing, xxiv
unhewn wood (*see also* sim-
    plicity; simplify), 15, 28,
    32, 37, 88, 89, 95
utopia, xxxi

valley (*see also* canyon), xxvi, 6,
    15, 28, 42, 69, 95
vessel (*see also* tilting vessel),
    9, 11, 28, 44, 90
village, 57
virtue (*see also* de; power), xvi,
    xxv–xxvi, xxix, 23, 44, 52,
    54, 57–58, 63, 66, 82, 88,
    93, 94, 96, 97, 99
  constant, 28
  deeply accumulating, 62
  enigmatic, 10, 54, 68, 93
  highest, 41
  lowest, 41
  of non-contention, 71
  outward appearance, 21
  power of, 57, 60, 99
vision, enigmatic, 10
vital energies, 10, 45, 58,
    86–87, 92, 94

Wagner, Rudolf G., xxx
Waley, Arthur, 85–86, 90, 93,
    95, 96, 97, 98, 99, 103,
    105, 107, 109, 110, 112–13
Wang Bi 王弼, xvi, xxx, 98
war, xvii, xxxi, 31, 72
war horses, 49

About the Translator

Philip J. Ivanhoe is Reader-Professor of Philosophy, City University of Hong Kong. His publications include *Confucian Moral Self Cultivation* (Hackett, 2000); *Virtue, Nature, and Moral Agency in the Xunzi* (Hackett, 2000), co-edited with T. C. Kline, III; *Ethics in the Confucian Tradition* (Hackett, 2002); *Essays on the Moral Philosophy of Mengzi* (Hackett, 2002), co-edited with Xiusheng Liu; and *Readings in Classical Chinese Philosophy* (Hackett, 2003), co-edited with Bryan W. Van Norden.